# Drink Pink!

Cocktails Inspired by **BARBIE, MEAN GIRLS, LEGALLY BLONDE,** and More

**Rhiannon Lee**
and **Georgie Glass**

Skyhorse Publishing

Interior photos by Georgie Glass on pages 20, 22, 24, 28, 30, 32, 38, 44, 48, 50, 52, 54, 56, 62, 64, 70, 82, 86, 88, 98, 102, 108, 116, 118, 120, 124, 126, 132, 134, 154, 160; photos by Aline Shaw on pages 68, 152; photos by Getty Images on pages 26, 36, 40, 42, 60, 74, 76, 78, 80, 92, 94, 104, 112, 128, 130, 140, 144, 146, 150, 164

Drinks styling by Grace Hatley on pages 20, 22, 24, 28, 30, 32, 38, 44, 48, 50, 52, 54, 56, 62, 64, 70, 82, 86, 88, 98, 102, 108, 116, 118, 120, 124, 126, 132, 134, 154, 160

Skyhorse Publishing books may be purchased in bulk at special discounts for sales promotion, corporate gifts, fund-raising, or educational purposes. Special editions can also be created to specifications. For details, contact the Special Sales Department, Skyhorse Publishing, 307 West 36th Street, 11th Floor, New York, NY 10018 or info@skyhorsepublishing.com.

Skyhorse® and Skyhorse Publishing® are registered trademarks of Skyhorse Publishing, Inc.®, a Delaware corporation.

Visit our website at www.skyhorsepublishing.com.
Please follow our publisher Tony Lyons on Instagram @tonylyonsisuncertain.

10 9 8 7 6 5 4 3 2 1

Library of Congress Cataloging-in-Publication Data on file.

Cover design by Brian Peterson
Cover photograph by Georgie Glass
Interior design by Chris Schultz

Print ISBN: 978-1-5107-8181-8
Ebook ISBN: 978-1-5107-8250-1

Printed in China

# CONTENTS

# INTRODUCTION

*Drink Pink!* is the essential accessory for any themed party or movie marathon. Within these pages, you'll discover expertly crafted pairings of delicious cocktails with iconic chick flick royalty! Get ready to sip, savor, and sparkle your way through iconic moments and unforgettable characters that have not only entertained us but also shaped and inspired us. From the chic streets of New York City with Carrie Bradshaw to the hallowed halls of Harvard with Elle Woods, each cocktail featured in this book pays homage to an iconic chick flick.

While the term "chick flick" is often unfairly dismissed as frivolous in the movie industry, this book is here to celebrate and toast this often-underappreciated genre of film. In a world where few movies pass the feminist barometer, the Bechdel test—featuring at least two named women characters who talk to each other about something other than a man—this female-led genre is all about friendships, self-discovery, and empowerment, all wrapped up in a glittering pink bow!

We all have a few cherished chick flicks we can't help but watch again and again. Whether it's a movie you watched with your besties at a slumber party growing up or a film from a first date with a special someone, there are some movies that stay with us throughout the years.

So, whether you're in need of the perfect pick-me-up for a girls' night out, planning a bachelorette party extravaganza, or craving a tasty treat for a mega movie marathon, this book is your go-to source for all things fabulous and pink-themed!

With easy-to-follow recipes and tips for stylish presentation, you will be able to elevate your cocktail game and impress even the most discerning guests. So go ahead, unleash your inner mixologist, and let your imagination run wild as you craft cocktails that are as stunning as they are delicious. Grab a cocktail shaker, put on some sequins, and raise a glass to pink drinks, chick flicks, movie magic, and girl power! Let the cocktail party begin!

# Basic Equipment

Lights, camera, cocktail! Just like a movie set needs its essential equipment to create cinematic magic, crafting the perfect cocktail also requires a set of essential tools. Whether you're a seasoned mixologist or a cocktail-curious chick-flick buff, having the right equipment is key to shaking, stirring, and sipping your way to cocktail perfection.

## Cocktail shaker
Coming in all different shapes and sizes, the standard shaker is stainless steel with three parts: a base known as a "can," a built-in strainer, and a cap (which can be used as a jigger). It's brilliantly straightforward and easy to keep clean. If you can't get hold of a cocktail shaker, consider using a large glass jar with a lid and a waterproof seal.

## Strainer
Most cocktail shakers are sold with a built-in strainer. However, if yours doesn't have one, then a flour sieve works just as well. (Tip: When a cocktail calls for straining, ensure you've used full ice cubes, as crushed ice tends to clog the strainer in standard shakers.)

## Jigger/shot glass
Something to measure your proportions with is a toolbox essential for any avid cocktail maker. The jigger is the standard measure for spirits and liqueurs. If you don't have a jigger, a single shot glass or even an eggcup can be a stand-in. In this book, one shot is measured as 1 ounce/30 milliliters (see page 165 for unit conversion).

## Muddler
To extract maximum flavor from certain fresh garnishes, such as mint or fruit, a muddler is used to crush the ingredients. If you are short a muddler, a fork with some gentle poking is a good substitute.

*(Continued on next page)*

## Bar spoon
The classic bar spoon has a long, twisted handle, a flat end, and a teardrop-shaped spoon used for measuring out and stirring spirits.

## Citrus squeezer
When making cocktails using fresh citrus, a citrus squeezer can really save time and ensure you get every last drop. If you don't have a squeezer, simply use your hands. (Tip: To get the most juice, roll the fruit in the palm of your hands then slice it in half and microwave for 5 seconds. Then simply use a fork to squeeze juice out.)

## Blender
An electric blender is required for some recipes involving fruit and ice cubes. It doesn't need to be an expensive or powerful blender, just good enough to crush ice.

# How To

From mastering the art of twisting citrus garnishes to delicately layering ingredients for that Instagram-worthy gradient effect, we'll guide you through the techniques needed to shake, layer, and stir your way to cocktail perfection.

## SHAKE

When a cocktail contains eggs, fruit juice, or cream, it is necessary to shake all the ingredients. It not only mixes the ingredients but chills them simultaneously. When shaking a cocktail, there is no agreement on the perfect time, but ten seconds of vigorous shaking is recommended.

## LAYER

Some drinks call for the careful layering of ingredients on top of each other to create an gradient effect. Always start with the heaviest liquid (with the most sugar content). To add a second layer, place a spoon upside down inside the glass, but not touching the first layer of alcohol. Very slowly pour the second liquid over the spoon. Repeat for any subsequent layers.

## STIR

Using a bar spoon, stir gently and deftly with ice to chill the concoction. When condensation forms on the outside of the glass, it is ready to drink.

## RIM

To add an elegant touch to your cocktail, you can decorate the rim of the glass with various ingredients like salt, sugar, cinnamon, and edible glitter. To achieve this, spread a few tablespoons of the desired ingredient onto a small plate. Moisten the outer rim of the glass with a citrus wedge, water, or a syrup, then roll the outer rim of the glass on the plate until lightly coated. Hold the glass upside down and tap to release any excess.

*(Continued on next page)*

## TWIST

Some cocktails call for a citrus twist to garnish a cocktail. This is a simple way to make a cocktail look elegant, but also adds citrus notes to the aroma of the drink. Use a sharp paring knife to cut a thin, oval disk of the peel avoiding the pith (the white spongy part). Gently grasp the outer edges skin-side down between the thumb and two fingers, and pinch the twist over the drink. Rub the peel around the rim of the glass, then drop it into the drink.

## IGNITE

Igniting cocktails is one of the most captivating and theatrical techniques in mixology. This fiery flourish not only adds a dramatic flair to the drink but also imparts unique flavors and aromas, elevating the entire drinking experience. High-proof spirits like overproof rum are the perfect choice for creating these fiery concoctions at room temperature. Due to the high density of the spirit, you can "float" it on top of a drink without mixing, achieved by carefully pouring the high-proof alcohol over the back of a spoon against the side of the glass. When applying a flame to the spirit, always ensure to keep your hands and any other flammable materials safely out of the way. Remember, never consume a lit drink; always wait until the flames have extinguished.

# GUIDE TO GLASSWARE

### COLLINS GLASS
These tall and narrow glasses originally get their name from collins gin drinks, but are now commonly used for a vast array of mixed drinks.

### MARTINI GLASS
As the name might suggest this glass was designed with a particular cocktail in mind. These triangle-bowl long stem glasses are used for a wide-range of straight-up (without ice) cocktails.

### GOBLET (BRANDY GLASS)
These large tulip-shaped glasses with a short stem are designed for brandy and cognac. The large bowl shape allows for the optimal air intake to bring out the flavors of the alcohol.

### ROCKS GLASS
This old-fashioned glass is a short tumbler with a wide base and top, typically associated with whiskey cocktails. The glass was designed to withstand muddling and hold large cubes of ice.

### COUPE
This saucer-shaped stemmed glass, rumored to have been originally designed after the shape of Marie Antoinette's breast, is traditionally used for serving champagne. However, the wide mouth is not great for containing bubbles and it is now more commonly used for cocktails without ice.

*(Continued on next page)*

### CHAMPAGNE FLUTE

This tall tulip-shaped glass is designed to show off the magical bubbles of the wine as they burst against the glass. They are great for any cocktail made with sparkling wine.

### HURRICANE GLASS

A tall, elegantly cut glass named after its hurricane-lamp-like shape, used for exotic/tropical drinks.

### MARGARITA GLASS

This glass was designed with one drink in mind. The distinctive double-bowl shape works particularly well for frozen margaritas. The wide rim makes it easy to add a salt or sugar rim.

### SHOT GLASS

Used for "shooting" a drink, these small glasses are used for a straight pour of a spirit.

### WINEGLASS

Wineglasses are not just for wine but are used in wine-based cocktails too.

# INGREDIENTS

## BITTERS
Bitters are concentrated alcoholic beverages infused with herbs, roots, and fruits, used to add depth and complexity to cocktails. They serve as flavor enhancers and aromatic agents, added in small quantities due to their intense flavor. Some commonly used bitters include Angostura bitters, known for its spicy and aromatic profile; Peychaud's Bitters, offering a lighter, anise-flavored touch; and orange bitters, which add a citrusy zest. These bitters are essential for creating well-balanced and flavorful cocktails.

## BUTTERFLY PEA FLOWER
Available online (we recommend b'Lure flower extract) or in certain kitchenware stores, this relatively unknown ingredient will turn drinks from blue to purple, and then pink with only a few drops! Used in traditional medicine and as a food coloring throughout Asia, this unique ingredient acts as a natural litmus test, changing color with the acidity of a drink.

## CITRUS JUICES
Lemon, lime, or grapefruit juice can be found in the vast majority of cocktails. These ingredients offer an acidic element that counterbalances sweetness to give a cocktail a well-balanced flavor profile. It is always preferable to use freshly squeezed citrus juice when making a cocktail.

## EDIBLE SHIMMER
Edible drink shimmers are now widely available in a wide range of colors and flavors and are a great way to turn an ordinary-looking cocktail into an extraordinary one! As far as this book is concerned, you can never have too much glitter!

(Continued on next page)

## EGGS

Several cocktails in this book incorporate egg whites to enhance viscosity and create a frothy foam by trapping air bubbles. However, if you are vegan, aquafaba (the water from a can of chickpeas) can be used as a substitute for egg whites.

## FLAVORED SYRUP

Flavored syrups are a simple way to add a new twist to a cocktail. Although many are commercially available, they are simple enough to make at home (recipes begin on page 11).

## INFUSED ALCOHOL

Infusing flavors into clear alcohols (like vodka, gin, white rum, and white tequila), is a delightful way to customize and elevate cocktails. The process is simple and allows for endless experimentation. To start, choose your desired flavoring agents, such as fresh fruits, herbs, candies, or spices. For example, try infusing vodka with fresh berries for a fruity twist, or add herbs like basil or rosemary for a more herbal note. You can also experiment with spices like cinnamon or vanilla beans to create warm and aromatic infusions perfect for festive drinks.

To infuse, simply add your chosen ingredients to a clean glass jar and pour in the clear alcohol. Seal the jar tightly and let it sit at room temperature for at least a few days to a week, shaking it occasionally to help release the flavors. The longer you let it infuse, the stronger the flavor will be, so be sure to taste-test along the way to achieve your desired intensity. Once infused, strain the vodka through a fine-mesh sieve or cheesecloth to remove the solids, and your flavored alcohol is ready to use in your favorite cocktails. Get creative and discover what combinations resonate best with your taste buds!

# HOMEMADE SYRUPS

Custom cocktail syrups are one of those special ingredients that can magically transform a drink. Whether it's basic simple syrup or a seasonal flavor combination (such as vanilla syrup, or something fruity like passion fruit syrup), you can easily make and enjoy it at home! Remember to take care and use sensible safety measures when working with heated sugar. Once made, syrups can be stored in the refrigerator for up to one month.

## SIMPLE SYRUP

Sometimes referred to as sugar syrup, this simple-to-create cocktail staple is basically a supersaturated mixture of sugar and water. The most common version uses two parts sugar to one part water (2:1). To make it, add the sugar and water to a small saucepan and heat at a medium heat until all the sugar is dissolved. Then, remove the syrup from the heat and allow it to cool.

## HONEY SYRUP

- ½ cup (100 milliliters) honey
- ½ cup (100 milliliters) water

Honey syrup, or liquid honey, is easy to make; combine equal parts honey with water in a saucepan, heat until dissolved (no more than a minute). Strain the syrup once cool into a jar or bottle and seal tightly with a lid.

*(Continued on next page)*

## LAVENDER SYRUP

- ½ cup (100 grams) sugar
- ½ cup (100 milliliters) water
- 2 teaspoons dried culinary lavender flowers

In a small saucepan, combine the water with the sugar and 2 tablespoons of dried culinary lavender. Bring to a simmer over medium heat, stirring occasionally, until the sugar has dissolved. Remove from heat and let it simmer for 10–15 minutes. Remove the mixture from the heat and allow to cool slightly before straining the syrup through a fine-mesh sieve into a clean container. Discard the solids. Allow the syrup to cool completely before transferring it to a glass bottle or jar for storage.

## STRAWBERRY SYRUP

- ⅓ pound (130 grams) fresh strawberries
- ½ cup (130 milliliters) water
- ⅓ cup (65 grams) sugar

Rince the strawberries, remove the stems, and slice them into smaller pieces. Place the strawberry pieces into a small saucepan, cover with the water and sugar, and slowly bring to a boil. Stir the mixture over medium heat until the sugar has completely dissolved. Once dissolved, bring the mixture to a gentle boil, then reduce the heat to low and let it simmer for about 10–15 minutes, or until the strawberries have softened and released their juices. Remove the mixture from the heat and let it cool slightly before straining the syrup through a fine-mesh sieve into a clean container, pressing on the strawberries to extract as much liquid as possible. Discard the solids. Allow the syrup to cool completely before transferring it to a glass bottle or jar for storage.

## Raspberry Syrup

- ⅓ pound (130 grams) fresh raspberries
- ½ cup (130 milliliters) water
- ⅓ cup (65 grams) sugar

Place the rinsed raspberries into a small saucepan, cover with the water and sugar, and slowly bring to a boil. Stir the mixture over medium heat until the sugar has completely dissolved. Once dissolved, bring the mixture to a gentle boil, then reduce the heat to low and let it simmer for about 10–15 minutes, or until the raspberries have softened and released their juices. Remove the mixture from the heat and let it cool slightly before straining the syrup through a fine-mesh sieve into a clean container, pressing on the raspberries to extract as much liquid as possible. Discard the solids. Allow the syrup to cool completely before transferring it to a glass bottle or jar for storage.

## Thyme Syrup

- ½ cup (100 grams) sugar
- ½ cup (100 milliliters) water
- 4–5 sprigs thyme

In a small saucepan over low heat, combine the sugar and water. Stir the mixture until the sugar is completely dissolved. Once dissolved, add a handful of fresh thyme sprigs to the saucepan and bring the mixture to a gentle boil. Reduce the heat to low and let the syrup simmer for about 10–15 minutes, allowing the thyme to infuse its aromatic flavor into the syrup. After simmering, remove the saucepan from the heat and let the syrup cool for a few minutes. Strain the syrup through a fine-mesh sieve into a clean container, pressing gently on the thyme to extract as much flavor as possible. Discard the thyme sprigs and let the syrup cool completely before transferring it to a glass bottle or jar for storage.

*(Continued on next page)*

## Passion Fruit Syrup

- ½ cup (100 grams) sugar
- ½ cup (130 milliliters) water
- 4 ripe passion fruits

In a small saucepan over low heat, combine the sugar and water. Stir occasionally until the sugar has completely dissolved, then remove from heat. Slice passion fruits in half and scoop out the pulp into the simple syrup. Let the fruit simmer in the syrup for 2 hours. Strain the solution through a fine mesh sieve. To avoid a cloudy simple syrup, don't press on the solids; let the syrup drain naturally. Discard any solids and let the syrup cool completely before transferring it to a glass bottle or jar for storage.

## Vanilla Syrup

- ½ cup (100 grams) sugar
- ½ cup (130 milliliters) water
- 1 teaspoon vanilla extract

In a small saucepan over low heat, combine the sugar and water. Stir occasionally until the sugar has completely dissolved, then remove from heat. As the simple syrup is cooling, stir in the vanilla extract. Allow the syrup to cool completely before transferring it to a glass bottle or jar for storage.

# GARNISHES

Garnishes can make a cocktail look so gorgeous that you won't be able to stop yourself from flaunting it all over social media. However, the significance of a garnish extends far beyond its aesthetic charm; the aroma and flavor it imparts can elevate a cocktail to new heights.

## CITRUS

Citrus garnishes add a refreshing brightness to any cocktail, elevating its flavor profile with a burst of acidity. Whether it's a classic twist of lemon adorning a gin and tonic, or a vibrant wedge of lime perched atop a margarita, citrus garnishes are the stars of the show, stealing scenes with their zesty allure.

## EDIBLE GLITTER

When it comes to edible glitters, the rule is simple: always add sparkle! Edible glitters are a must-have for any girls' night cocktail party, effortlessly transforming drinks into dazzling spectacles. Simply sprinkle a pinch of glitter over the finished drink or rim the glass with a shimmering coat for an extra touch of sparkle. Widely available in a range of colors, there is always reason or season that a little extra sparkle would not go amiss.

## EDIBLE FLOWERS

Flowers bring a fresh botanical touch to many cocktails (as well as being super Instagramable) and can be purchased at certain grocery stores or cake decorating supply stores. The most commonly used edible flowers in cocktail making are cornflowers, nasturtium, pansies, lavender, orchids, dandelions, and violets, to name a few.

*(Continued on next page)*

## FRUIT

Fresh fruits like berries and tropical fruits not only add vibrant colors and visual appeal to your drinks but also infuse them with a burst of natural sweetness, acidity, or aromatic oils. Whether you're garnishing a sophisticated martini with a delicate cherry or adding a tropical flair to a rum-based cocktail with a slice of pineapple or a wedge of mango, the right fruit garnish can transform a good cocktail into an exceptional one.

## HERBS

Herb garnishes are often used in cocktail making. The most frequently used in this book is mint, as it not only looks pretty but adds a sweet refreshing aroma, too. To get the most out of mint, always place the leaves flat between your palms and clap to release their essential oils. Other herbs commonly used are thyme, basil, and more.

## INEDIBLE FLOURISH

An inedible garnish can play a starring role in bringing your cinematic cocktails to life. These playful and thematic garnishes not only look fabulous but also add a fun and whimsical touch to your cocktail creations. Embrace the tropical holiday vibes with cocktail umbrellas or add some Hollywood "wow" factor with an indoor sparkler. The possibilities are endless, so unleash your creativity and let your imagination run wild!

## SAVORY GARNISHES

A few of the cocktails in the book call for savory garnishes like celery and olives. This is possibly one of the best ways to get your five veggies a day.

# COCKTAILS

# Drink Pink! It Goes with Everything!

This chapter is dedicated to the world's most famous plastic doll with a collection of cocktails that are as vibrant, fun, and stylish as the iconic doll herself! From classic Barbie-inspired pink hues to playful garnishes and dazzling presentation, each drink in this chapter is designed to capture the essence of her chic and glamorous world.

Just like Barbie, these cocktails are all about fun and self-expression. Experiment to discover the styles and flavors that best suit you. Whether you're sipping on a Barbie-inspired Malibu Dream Drink or a Pink Cadillac Cosmo, each drink promises to transport you to a world of glitz, where every moment is an opportunity to shine.

So, grab your favorite pink accessories, gather your gal pals, and get ready to celebrate the ultimate icon of femininity and fun, Barbie!

# Barbie-Inspired Malibu Dream Drink

Introducing the "Malibu Dream Drink"—the ultimate Barbie-themed cocktail that's as fabulous as it is fun! This refreshing concoction is a tropical vacation in a glass, making it the perfect accessory for a hot summer's day or a stroll along the beach. So, dust off your pink stilettos, grab your sunglasses, and get ready to soak up some of that Malibu sun.

**Serves 1**
**Preparation time: 5 minutes**
**Glassware: Hurricane glass**

1½ ounces (45 milliliters) Malibu coconut rum

2 ounces (60 milliliters) pineapple juice

1 ounce (30 milliliters) cranberry juice

1 ounce (30 milliliters) fresh orange juice

Drizzle grenadine

Ice cubes

*Garnish:* Pink sugar (sugar combined with pink food coloring) and a pineapple wedge

1. With a mortar and pestle, grind the sugar with the pink food coloring. Rim the glass using grenadine syrup and pink sugar (learn how to rim a glass on page 5).

2. In a cocktail shaker, combine the Malibu coconut rum, pineapple juice, cranberry juice, fresh orange juice, and grenadine along with a handful of ice cubes and shake vigorously until the mixture is cool.

3. Carefully strain the mixture into the prepared rimmed glass.

4. Garnish with a pineapple wedge.

# Mojo Dojo Mojito

*Just like Ken in his Mojo Dojo Casa House, this cocktail classic just got a whole lot spicier! This drink is the perfect balance of ridiculously hot and charmingly refreshing, much like the horse-loving Beach Professional himself.*

**Serves 1**
**Preparation time: 5 minutes**
**Glassware: Collins glass**

2 ounces (60 milliliters) light rum

1 ounce (30 milliliters) fresh lime juice

1 ounce (30 milliliters) simple syrup (see page 11)

4–6 fresh mint leaves

1 small jalapeño pepper, thinly sliced (adjust for spice level)

½ lime, cut into wedges

Soda water (to top up)

Ice cubes

*Garnish:* Lime slices and additional jalapeño slices

1. In a sturdy glass or cocktail shaker, place the fresh mint leaves and thinly sliced jalapeño pepper and muddle the ingredients to release their flavors.

2. Add the muddled ingredients to the glass and fill with ice cubes, almost to the top.

3. Next combine the light rum, lime juice, and simple syrup and use a cocktail stirrer or a long spoon to gently mix the ingredients together.

4. Top up the glass with soda water before garnishing with a lime wedge and a few extra slices of jalapeño.

# Just Beach

*If, like Ken, you are destined to "just beach" in life, then this is the cocktail for you! At its core, this tequila sunset cocktail combines the bold kick of tequila with the sweetness of the fresh orange juice and grenadine. With a gorgeous gradient of colors in the glass you can picture the sun setting over the horizon and all your troubles just melt away in another perfect day in Barbieland.*

**Serves 1**
**Preparation time: 5 minutes**
**Glassware: Hurricane glass**

2 teaspoons grenadine

1¾ ounces (50 milliliters) silver tequila

1 ounce (30 milliliters) fresh lemon juice

4 ounces (120 milliliters) orange juice

1 ounce (30 milliliters) triple sec

Ice cubes

Orange juice (to top up)

*Garnish:* Miniature sparkler, orange wedge, strawberries, and two glacé cherries on a cocktail stick

1. Pour the grenadine into the base of the glass and set aside.

2. Combine the tequila, triple sec, and citrus juices in a cocktail shaker along with a handful of ice cubes and shake vigorously until the mixture is cool.

3. Add ice cubes into the hurricane glass and then carefully strain the cocktail, while being careful not to disturb the grenadine layer.

4. Add more ice to fill the glass and top up with extra orange juice if needed.

5. Garnish with an orange wedge and two glacé cherries. For the final flourish, secure a miniature sparkler in the strawberry and light before serving. Remove and safely dispose of the spent sparkler before drinking!

# Pink Cadillac Cosmo

*Get ready to cruise into cocktail heaven with the Pink Cadillac Cosmo! This luxurious libation is a twist on the classic pink cosmopolitan cocktail. With a vibrant blend of raspberry vodka, triple sec, and cranberry juice, this cocktail delivers a refreshing burst of flavor with every sip. So, get ready to drive guests wild with this glass of pink perfection.*

**Serves 1**
**Preparation time: 5 minutes:**
**Glassware: Martini glass**

Drizzle grenadine

1½ ounces (45 milliliters) raspberry vodka

1 ounce (30 milliliters) triple sec

½ ounce (15 milliliters) fresh lime juice

½ ounce (15 milliliters) white cranberry juice

Ice cubes

*Garnish:* Pink sugar (sugar combined with pink food coloring) and a fresh raspberry

1. With a mortar and pestle, grind the sugar with the pink food coloring. Rim the glass using grenadine and pink sugar (learn how to rim a glass on page 5).

2. Combine the vodka, triple sec, and juices in a cocktail shaker along with a handful of ice cubes. Shake vigorously until the mixture is cool.

3. Carefully strain the mixture into the rimmed martini glass and garnish with a fresh raspberry.

# Pink Lady

*Like the inspirational lady in pink herself, this classic cocktail has a long history and was a favorite among Hollywood stars of the golden years such as blonde-bombshell Jayne Mansfield. While the sweetness from the grenadine and lightness from the frothy egg white may give off a delicate impression, don't be deceived—this cocktail packs quite a punch with the gin and brandy. So, enjoy sipping on this gorgeous pink drink and let it bring some old school Hollywood glamor and sparkle to your night.*

**Serves 1**
**Preparation time: 5 minutes**
**Glassware: Coupe**

2 ounces (60 milliliters) gin

1 ounce (30 milliliters) apple brandy

¾ ounce (25 milliliters) fresh lemon juice

½ ounce (15 milliliters) grenadine

½ ounce (15 milliliters) egg white

Ice cubes

*Garnish:* Edible viola flowers and a pinch of edible glitter

1. Combine the gin, apple brandy, fresh lemon juice, grenadine, and egg white in a cocktail shaker along with a handful of ice cubes. Shake until cold and the egg white is frothy.

2. Carefully strain the mixture into a coupe. Garnish by carefully floating some edible flowers on the cocktail foam and a dusting of edible glitter.

# Rosy Dreams

Put on your rose-colored glasses and step into a dreamy Barbie-inspired realm with this enchanting Rosy Dreams cocktail. This exquisite concoction seamlessly merges the sophistication of rose-infused gin, with its delicate floral notes, and the playfulness of cotton candy, creating a drink fit for a modern-day Barbie. It's the perfect drink for a girls' night out, a bridal shower, or any celebration where elegance and fun collide.

**Serves 1**
**Preparation time: 5 minutes**
**Glassware: Coupe**

1 ounce (30 milliliters) rose-infused gin

½ ounce (15 milliliters) crème de cacao

⅓ ounce (10 milliliters) fresh lemon juice

⅓ ounce (10 milliliters) rose water

½ ounce (15 milliliters) egg white

Ice cubes

*Garnish:* Cotton candy cloud and edible glitter

1. Combine all the ingredients in a cocktail shaker along with a handful of ice cubes and shake vigorously until the mixture is cool.

2. Carefully strain the cocktail into a coupe and garnish with a cotton candy cloud, a pinch of edible glitter, and a few dried rose petals.

# Glitter Ball

*No Barbie-themed viewing party is complete without a giant blowout after-party, with planned choreography and a bespoke themed cocktail! So, throw on your sequined mirror ball jumpsuit and let this cocktail help you dance the night away!*

**Serves 1**
**Preparation time: 5 minutes**
**Glassware: Martini glass**

2 ounces (60 milliliters) pink gin

1 ounce (30 milliliters) elderflower liqueur

1 ounce (30 milliliters) cranberry juice

½ ounce (15 milliliters) fresh lime juice

½ ounce (15 milliliters) simple syrup (see page 11)

Edible pink glitter

Ice cubes

*Garnish:* Glittery raspberry on a cocktail stick

1. Rim a martini glass with water and edible pink glitter (learn how to rim a glass on page 5).

2. Combine the pink gin, elderflower liqueur, cranberry juice, fresh lime juice, simple syrup, and a pinch of edible glitter in a cocktail shaker along with a handful of ice cubes and shake vigorously until the mixture is cool.

3. Carefully strain the mixture into the rimmed glass.

4. To garnish, start by washing a raspberry. While it's still moist, gently roll it in edible pink glitter. Then, carefully place the glitter-coated raspberry on the cocktail using a cocktail stick.

# Blonde Bombshell Martini

*Step into the iconic pink stilettos of the ultimate blonde bombshell, Barbie, and sip in style with the Blonde Bombshell Martini! Inspired by Greta Gerwig's blockbuster movie, this cocktail reminds us that in a world where Barbie can be anything, why not be a mixologist? Shake up some martini magic with this exquisite blend of vanilla vodka and white chocolate and conquer the world one sip at a time.*

**Serves 1**
**Preparation time: 5 minutes**
**Glassware: Martini glass**

1 tablespoon maple syrup for decorating the glass

2 ounces (60 milliliters) vanilla vodka

1 ounce (30 milliliters) white chocolate liqueur

1 ounce (30 milliliters) coconut cream

½ ounce (15 milliliters) simple syrup (see page 11)

Dash lemon juice

Ice cubes

*Garnish:* Shredded coconut (for rimming) and a lemon twist

1. Rim a martini glass (learn how to rim a glass on page 5) with the shredded coconut and maple syrup.

2. Combine the vanilla vodka, white chocolate liqueur, coconut cream, simple syrup, and a dash of lemon juice in a cocktail shaker along with a handful of ice cubes and shake vigorously until the mixture is cool.

3. Carefully strain the cocktail into your coconut-rimmed martini glass and garnish with a lemon twist.

# TIPSY TEENAGE DREAMS

From the halls of high school drama to the pangs of first love, these films captured the essence of our bygone adolescence like no other. In this chapter, we celebrate the highs and lows of teenage life, all while exploring the delicious concoctions inspired by beloved movies such as *Mean Girls*, *To All the Boys I've Loved Before*, and *The Princess Diaries*.

Whether you resonated with the queen bee vibes of Regina George or the awkward charm of Princess Mia Thermopolis, this chapter is a celebration of the diversity of teenage experiences. After all, in the realm of adulthood, we're all royalty in our own right.

So, let's kick back, relax, and reminisce of teenage days gone by. Whether you faced the anxiety-inducing pressure of AP calculus exams like Kady or experienced heartbreaks that felt like the end of the world like Lara Jean, each experience in our formative years shaped us into the strong individuals we are today.

# On Wednesdays, We Drink Pink!

*Get ready to infuse your Wednesday nights with a splash of sass and a dose of pink with On Wednesdays, We Drink Pink!, a riff on the classic Paloma but with a vibrant, pink twist. Whether you're hitting the town with your girl squad or you're planning the ultimate Mean Girls movie night, this is the cocktail for you. So, dress to impress in pink, channel your inner Regina George, and let this cocktail kick-start a fabulous night!*

**Serves 1**
**Preparation time: 5 minutes:**
**Glassware: Collins glass**

1¾ ounces (50 milliliters) reposado tequila

⅓ ounce (10 milliliters) fresh lime juice

⅓ ounce (10 milliliters) honey syrup (see page 11)

2 ounces (60 milliliters) pink grapefruit juice

Soda water (to top up)

Ice cubes

*Garnish:* Sea salt and a pink grapefruit wedge

1. Rim a collins glass (learn how to rim a glass on page 5) using sea salt and water.

2. Combine the tequila, fresh lime juice, honey syrup, and a pink grapefruit juice in a cocktail shaker along with a handful of ice cubes and shake vigorously until the mixture is cool.

3. Carefully strain the mixture into the prepared rimmed glass.

4. Add a few ice cubes and top up with soda water and garnish with a grapefruit wedge.

# You Can't Sip with Us!

*Indulge in the essence of the Plastics with this bubbly and bold cocktail. Don't let the sweetness from the honey syrup or its bubbly nature deceive you! Beneath its rosy façade lies the zesty punch of grapefruit and the subtle heat of ginger. Follow these simple guidelines to craft the perfect drink, ideal for sharing gossip within your own clique. But remember, failure to adhere to these instructions means "You can't sip with us!"*

### Serves 1
### Preparation time: 10 minutes
### Glassware: Wineglass

2 ounces (60 milliliters) pink gin

1 ounce (30 milliliters) grapefruit juice

1 ounce (30 milliliters) fresh lime juice

1 ounce (30 milliliters) honey syrup (see page 11)

¼ inch fresh ginger, grated

Sparkling water (to top up)

Ice cubes

*Garnish:* Pink grapefruit wedge

1. Start by preparing the honey syrup.

2. In the can of the cocktail shaker, muddle the grated ginger and the honey syrup together.

3. Combine the pink gin, grapefruit juice, and fresh lime juice in a cocktail shaker with a handful of ice cubes. Shake until the mixture is cool.

4. Strain the cocktail into a chilled wineglass.

5. Garnish the cocktail with a pink grapefruit wedge.

# Plastic Fantastic Punch

The Plastic Fantastic Punch is a total crowd-pleaser that steals the spotlight at any party it is served at! Presented in a watermelon half, this refreshing fusion of watermelon, vodka, and sparkling wine screams for a summer get-together! So, whether you're hosting a secret house party while your parents are away, or just chilling with friends on a sunny day, let this cocktail be the star of the show.

**Serves 6**
**Preparation time: 10 minutes**
**Glassware: Large pitcher and collins glasses**

1 small seedless watermelon

6 mint leaves

4 ounces (120 milliliters) vodka

1 ounce (30 milliliters) simple syrup (see page 11)

1 ounce (30 milliliters) fresh lemon juice

Sparkling wine (to top up)

Ice cubes

*Garnish:* Watermelon wedge

1. Cut a watermelon in half, and using a large spoon or ice cream scoop, carve out the inside and set it aside as the punch bowl.

2. Add the watermelon chunks, mint leaves, and a handful of ice to a blender and puree until smooth. Strain the puree into a container and discard any solid particles.

3. In the carved-out watermelon half, add two handfuls of ice, vodka, simple syrup, fresh lemon juice, and 5 ounces (150 milliliters) of watermelon-mint juice.

4. Top up with sparkling wine and serve in collins glasses garnished with watermelon wedges.

# Burn Book Bellini

*Just like in the girl-world of Mean Girls, where everything may seem fine and peachy on the surface, this tantalizing peach cocktail has a few secrets lurking among the bubbles. While the fruity peach puree is a refreshing way to enjoy some fruit, the schnapps kicks this cocktail up a notch and puts the "burn" into Burn Book Bellini. So, pour yourself a glass and let it all out, because just like prosecco, it's not good to keep these things bottled up!*

**Serves 1**
**Preparation time: 10 minutes**
**Glassware: Champagne flutes**

### For the peach puree:

4 medium white peaches (pitted and quartered)

3 ice cubes

1 teaspoon fresh lemon juice

¾ ounces (22 milliliters) simple syrup (see page 11)

### For the cocktail:

2 ounces (60 milliliters) peach puree

1 ounce (30 milliliters) peach schnapps

Prosecco (sparkling wine) (to top up)

Pinch edible gold glitter

*Garnish:* Peach slice and mint leaves

1. For the peach puree, add the pitted peaches, ice cubes, lemon juice, and simple syrup to a blender and blend until smooth. Pass the puree through a fine mesh to remove any of the larger pulp.

2. Next, pour the peach puree and peach schnapps into the glass, and slowly top up with prosecco (sparkling wine).

3. Add a pinch of golden edible glitter for that luxurious added touch and gently stir with a bar spoon to bring the drink together.

4. Garnish with a peach slice and mint leaves before serving.

# Humpday Treat

*Celebrate the midweek milestone just like Regina's mom with the Humpday Treat. These delicious shots are not like \*regular\* shots, they're \*cool\* shots with extra special rainbow sprinkles. Cheers to making Wednesdays a little sweeter!*

**Serves 5–6**
**Preparation time: 5 minutes**
**Glassware: Shot glasses**

1 tablespoon maple syrup for decorating the glass

1 ounce (30 milliliters) vanilla vodka

1 ounce (30 milliliters) Irish cream liqueur

1 ounce (30 milliliters) white chocolate liqueur

1 ounce (30 milliliters) amaretto liqueur

1 ounce (30 milliliters) light cream

Ice cubes

*Garnish:* Rainbow sprinkles and whipped cream

1. Rim the shot glasses (learn how to rim a glass on page 5) with maple syrup and rainbow sprinkles.

2. Combine the vanilla vodka, Irish cream liqueur, white chocolate liqueur, amaretto liqueur, and light cream in a cocktail shaker along with a handful of ice cubes and shake vigorously until the mixture is cool.

3. Carefully strain the mixture into the prepared rimmed shot glasses. Garnish each shot with a small flourish of whipped cream.

# You Go, Hot Cocoa!

*This pink hot chocolate concoction is the ultimate treat to cozying up under a blanket and rewatching this iconic movie. With a candy cane cocktail stirrer sent from the queen bee herself, this drink gains a refreshing minty twist as it dissolves. But beware, this cocktail is so irresistibly delicious, just like Glen, that you might find yourself indulging in four or more before the movie even ends.*

**Serves 2**
**Preparation time: 10 minutes**
**Glassware: Glass mugs**

2 ounces (60 milliliters) white chocolate liqueur

1 ounce (30 milliliters) raspberry liqueur

4 ounces (120 milliliters) hot milk

1 ounce (30 milliliters) whipped cream vodka

2–3 drops pink food coloring

*Garnish:* Whipped cream, mini pink marshmallows, and candy canes

1. Heat the milk in a pan until hot, but not boiling (microwave-safe container works too).

2. In a separate glass, combine the white chocolate liqueur, raspberry liqueur, and whipped cream vodka, adding a few drops of pink food coloring. Pour in the hot milk, stir, and top with whipped cream.

3. Sprinkle on mini pink marshmallows and add candy cane stirrers.

# Fetch Fizzy Frosé

The Fetch Fizzy Frosé reigns supreme as the apex predator of summer drinks, with a flavor as full-bodied as Gretchen Wieners's hair. With a blend of frozen rosé, the sweetness of strawberries, and a zesty twist of lemon, this eye-catching pink cocktail is sure to make others eager to join your cocktail clique. So, unlike the word "fetch," this cocktail is definitely going to be happening this summer!

**Serves 6–8**
**Preparation time: Overnight + 10 minutes**
**Glassware: Collins glasses**

1 bottle (750 milliliters) rosé

4 ounces (120 milliliters) strawberry syrup (see page 12)

2 ounces (60 milliliters) fresh lemon juice

Ice cubes

Sparkling water (to top up)

*Garnish:* Fresh strawberries and lemon wheels

1. Pour the bottle of rosé into a deep roasting tin and carefully put it in the freezer overnight. (Wine doesn't freeze solid so don't be concerned if yours is a little slushy.)

2. Prepare the strawberry syrup.

3. In a blender, combine the frozen rosé, strawberry syrup, and fresh lemon juice. Blend until the mixture is smooth and slushy.

4. Fill glasses with ice cubes and pour the Fetch Fizzy Frosé mixture over the ice, leaving enough room to top up each glass with a splash of sparkling water.

5. Garnish each cocktail with fresh strawberries and lemon wheels.

# Karen's Brain Freeze

*You don't have to have a fifth sense like Karen to know this cocktail is the perfect showstopper at any gal-pal dinner party. As sweet and whimsical as Karen herself, it blends together the fruity strawberry flavors with the rich Irish cream into a pink-hued frozen delight. Adorned with pink mini marshmallows and delicate pink meringues, this cocktail tastes as delicious as it looks.*

**Serves 8**
**Preparation time: 2 hours**
**Glassware: Collins glasses**

## Raspberry puree:

1 cup (125 grams) fresh raspberries, plus extra for serving

½ cup (100 grams) sugar

½ cup (100 grams) water

## For the cocktail:

1 ½ cup (300 grams) fresh strawberries, hulled

4–5 handfuls of ice cubes

8 ½ ounces (250 milliliters) Irish cream liqueur

4 ounces (120 milliliters) strawberry liqueur

*Garnish:* mint leaves, pink mini marshmallows, and mini pink meringues

1. In a small saucepan, combine the fresh raspberries, sugar, and water. Bring the mixture to a boil. Allow it to boil for 5 minutes, or until the mixture is reduced and thickened. Remove the saucepan from the heat and let it cool for a moment.

2. Using a blender or food processor, blend the raspberry puree ingredients until smooth. Put in the refrigerator for approximately 30 minutes, or until chilled.

3. While the raspberry puree is chilling, place eight collins glasses in the freezer to chill.

4. Drizzle about ¼ cup (60 milliliters) of the chilled raspberry puree down the inside of each chilled glass, swirling around to coat. Return the glasses to the freezer.

*(Continued on next page)*

5. Halve the remaining strawberries. In a blender, combine the halved strawberries, ice cubes, Irish cream liqueur, strawberry liqueur, and the remaining chilled raspberry puree. Blend the mixture until smooth with a slushy consistency.

6. Pour the strawberry slush mixture into the chilled glasses that have the raspberry drizzle.

7. Top each glass with pink mini marshmallows, mini pink swirl meringues, and a few fresh mint leaves.

# Genovian Orange Royale

*Step into the enchanting world of Genovia with the Genovian Orange Royale, a cocktail as delightful and regal as the princess herself. Crafted to honor the spirit of The Princess Diaries, this drink combines the elegance of royalty with a twist of excitement that only Mia could bring. Get your friends screaming "Shut up" in disbelief after tasting this totally delicious regal cocktail.*

**Serves 1**
**Preparation time: 10 minutes**
**Glassware: Wineglass**

½ ounce (15 milliliters) reposado tequila

½ ounce (15 milliliters) triple sec

½ ounce (15 milliliters) elderflower liqueur

½ ounce (15 milliliters) blood orange juice

½ ounce (15 milliliters) fresh lime juice

2 dashes orange bitters

Rosé champagne/ sparkling wine (to top up)

*Garnish:* Blood orange wheel

1. Combine the tequila, triple sec, elderflower liqueur, juices, and orange bitters in a cocktail shaker along with a handful of ice cubes and shake vigorously until the mixture is cool.

2. Carefully strain the mixture into the wineglass.

3. Top up the glass with chilled rosé champagne/sparkling wine and garnish with an orange wheel.

# Mean Margarita

Unleash your inner dragon with this Mean Margarita, a bold blend of pink dragon fruit and fiery tequila that's sure to spark some sassy gossip sessions. So, gather your squad, pour a glass, and channel your inner Damian and Janis as you plot revenge against those who've wronged you, all while enjoying this unforgettable cocktail. Whether you're dishing out compliments or throwing shade, the Mean Margarita is your go-to drink to fuel those gossip-filled evenings!

**Serves 2**
**Preparation time: 10 minutes**
**Glassware: Margarita glass**

1 pink dragon fruit

2 ounces (60 milliliters) fresh lime juice

3 ounces (90 milliliters) silver tequila

1 ounce (30 milliliters) triple sec

1 ounce (30 milliliters) honey syrup (see page 11)

Ice cubes

*Garnish:* 2 tablespoons salt, 1–2 drops of pink food coloring, and lime wheel

1. With a mortar and pestle, grind the salt with the pink food coloring. Rim the margarita glasses with pink salt and water (learn how to rim a glass on page 5).

2. Slice the dragon fruit in half and scoop out the flesh with a spoon.

3. In a blender combine the flesh of the dragon fruit with the lime juice, tequila, triple sec, honey syrup, and two handfuls of ice cubes. Blend until smooth.

4. Carefully pour the margarita into the prepared salt-rimmed margarita glasses.

5. Garnish each with a lime wheel.

# To All the Cocktails
# I've Loved Before

*Inspired by the heartwarming book and film series To All the Boys I've Loved Before, this cocktail is a sophisticated twist on the classic Love Letter cocktail. This enchanting libation captures the essence of sweet nostalgia and new beginnings, just like Lara Jean's unforgettable love letters.*

**Serves 1**
**Preparation time: 5 minutes**
**Glassware: Martini glass**

1 ounce (30 milliliters) bourbon

½ ounce (15 milliliters) triple sec

½ ounce (15 milliliters) egg white

7 dashes Angostura bitters

7 dashes Peychaud's Bitters

Champagne/sparkling wine (to top up)

Ice cubes

*Garnish:* Lemon twist

1. Combine the bourbon, triple sec, egg white, and bitters in a cocktail shaker along with a handful of ice cubes. Shake until cold and the egg white is frothy.

2. Carefully strain the mixture into a martini glass and top up with champagne/sparkling wine. Garnish with a lemon twist.

# Pom-Pom Punch

*Get ready to rally with this highly spirited cocktail, inspired by the fierce world of cheerleading and the iconic rivalry in the film franchise Bring It On. This drink is like the head cheerleader of cocktails—bold, confident, and totally in charge. So, grab your pom-poms, strike a pose, and let the cheer—and the shade—fly as you sip on this fierce and fabulous cocktail. Go team!*

**Serves 8**
**Preparation time: 10 minutes**
**Glassware: Large pitcher and rocks glasses**

12 ounces (350 milliliters) dark rum

34 ounces (1 liter) cranberry juice

34 ounces (1 liter) ginger ale

Ice cubes

*Garnish:* Pom-pom decorations

1. In a large pitcher filled with ice cubes, combine all the ingredients and give a good mix before serving.

2. Serve in rocks glasses garnished with a pom-pom stirrer.

# SORORITY SISTER SIPS

Immerse yourself in the spirit of female solidarity with the "Sorority Sister Sips" chapter, where we pay homage to the college experience through the lens of some of the best college chick flicks. Inspired by the spirited portrayals of college life in films like *Legally Blonde*, *Pitch Perfect*, and *The House Bunny*, this chapter is all about embracing fun, female friendships, and a fabulous cocktail or two!

From the classy sophistication of Elle Woods and the Delta Nu sorority sisters to the quirky charm of Shelly and her Zeta Alpha Zeta misfits, this chapter has a cocktail that's perfect for every college persona. However, be warned, after indulging in a few of these fabulous cocktails, you may find yourself struggling to recite the actual alphabet, let alone the Greek one!

# Totally Clueless

*Embodying the essence of Cher's impeccable taste, this cocktail is a refreshing, bubbly, and stylish delight, elevating any fashion-forward soirée to new heights of sophistication. With its fruity flavors and effervescent charm, it's the perfect accessory to have in hand as you mingle and make memories. You would have to be totally clueless to pass on this chic concoction!*

**Serves 1**
**Preparation time: 5 minutes**
**Glassware: Rocks glass**

1 ½ ounces (45 milliliters) vodka

2 ounces (60 milliliters) pomegranate juice

2 ounces (60 milliliters) fresh pink grapefruit juice

Soda water (to top up)

Ice cubes

*Garnish:* Pink grapefruit slices, pomegranate seeds, and mint leaves

1. Combine the vodka, pomegranate juice, and freshly squeezed grapefruit juice in a cocktail shaker along with a handful of ice cubes and shake vigorously until the mixture is cool.

2. Carefully strain the mixture into a glass filled with ice. Top up the glass with soda water.

3. Garnish the cocktail with a few pomegranate seeds, a slice of pink grapefruit, and a few mint leaves.

# Cher's Perfect Pout Punch

*Get ready to strike a pose with your besties, just like the reigning queens of Beverly Hills High School. This delightful cocktail not only tantalizes your taste buds, but also leaves you with a pout-worthy look that's Instagram-ready. Adorned with luscious red cherry lips and a sprinkling of popping candy, this drink is as sweet as the enduring friendship shared by Cher and Dionne in the iconic cult movie.*

**Serves 1**
**Preparation time: 5 minutes**
**Glassware: Martini glass**

2 ounces (60 milliliters) vodka

1 ounce (30 milliliters) cherry brandy

½ ounce (15 milliliters) fresh lemon juice

3 ounce (90 milliliters) cherry juice

Ice cubes

*Garnish:* Rim the glass with popping candy and add pink lip-shaped candy on a cocktail stick

1. Rim the martini glass with popping candy (learn how to rim a glass on page 5).

2. Combine the vodka, cherry brandy, fresh lime, and cherry juice in a cocktail shaker, along with a handful of ice cubes. Shake vigorously until the mixture is cool.

3. Carefully strain the mixture into the prepared rimmed martini glass and garnish with a cocktail stick with candy lips.

# Bend and Schnapps Shots

*Indulge in the ultimate pink party starter with our Bend and Schnapps Shots Inspired by the iconic "bend and snap" move from Legally Blonde, these shots are the perfect blend of fun and flirtation to elevate your evening. To master this playful technique, simply line up your shots, gracefully bend down, and snap them up in one fluid motion. With the right attitude, you'll not only captivate your crush but also enjoy an impressive 83 percent success rate in securing another round!*

**Serves 4**
**Preparation time: 5 minutes**
**Glassware: Shot glasses**

4 ounces (120 milliliters) vodka

2 ounces (60 milliliters) peach schnapps

2 ounces (60 milliliters) cranberry juice

Ice cubes

*Garnish:* Granulated sugar for decorating the shot glasses

1. Rim the shot glasses using water and granulated sugar (learn how to rim a glass on page 5).

2. Combine the vodka, peach schnapps, and cranberry juice in a cocktail shaker, along with a handful of ice cubes. Shake vigorously until the mixture is cool.

3. Strain the mixture into the prepared rimmed shot glasses.

# Bold Ambition

*Beneath its pretty facade, this bold cocktail has a complex and ambitious blend of flavors: spicy cardamom radiates warmth while a zesty undercurrent from grapefruit bitters tantalizes the taste buds. Both enhance the botanical flavors of the gin and the dry vermouth. This cocktail is truly not one to judge from first impressions. So, whether you're conquering the courtroom or simply celebrating life's victories, let this cocktail help you toast life's triumphs!*

**Serves 1**
**Preparation time: 5 minutes**
**Glassware: Coupe**

3 ounces (90 milliliters) gin

1 ounce (30 milliliters) dry vermouth

1 ounce (30 milliliters) elderflower liqueur

1 ounce (30 milliliters) fresh lemon juice

1 ounce (30 milliliters) simple syrup (see page 11)

3 dashes grapefruit bitters

3 dashes cardamom bitters

Ice cubes

*Garnish:* Lemon wedge

1. Combine all the ingredients in a cocktail shaker along with a handful of ice cubes and shake vigorously until the mixture is cool.

2. Carefully strain the cocktail into a coupe and garnish with a lemon wedge.

# Sorority Sister Sangria

*Welcome to the sisterhood of flavor with the enchanting "Sorority Sister Sangria" cocktail! Inspired by the camaraderie and vibrant energy of sororities featured in many classic chick flicks, this delightful concoction is the perfect blend of fun, friendship, and fabulous flavor. So, gather your sorority sisters, pour yourself a large glass, and celebrate fierce female friendships!*

**Serves 6–8**
**Preparation time: 10 minutes**
**Glassware: Pitcher and mason jars**

2 lemons (cut into thin slices)

2 limes (cut into thin slices)

1 orange (cut into thin slices)

Several coarsely torn mint leaves

6 ounces (180 milliliters) agave nectar syrup

5 ounces (120 milliliters) silver tequila

2 ounces (60 milliliters) fresh lime juice

1 bottle red wine

Soda water (to top up)

*Garnish:* Torn mint leaves

1. Combine the sliced fruit, mint leaves, agave nectar, tequila, lime juice, and red wine in a large pitcher.

2. Give the mixture a vigorous stir and top with soda water. Allow the cocktail to chill in the fridge for at least an hour before serving.

3. To serve, pour the cocktail into mason jars and garnish with torn mint leaves.

# Pitcher Perfect

*Prepare to channel your inner Pitch Perfect diva with the Pitcher Perfect cocktail! This bubbly, pink concoction is the ultimate refresher for your vocal cords after an impromptu a cappella showdown. Just like the Bellas, this drink hits all the right notes, delivering an aca-mazing taste sensation that's sure to dazzle your senses!*

**Serves 6–8**
**Preparation time: 5 minutes**
**Glassware: Large pitcher**

6 ounces (180 milliliters) vodka

2 ounces (60 milliliters) coconut rum

3 ounces (90 milliliters) fresh lime juice

3 ounces (90 milliliters) white cranberry juice

1.25 liters pink lemonade

Pinch edible glitter

Ice cubes

*Garnish:* Lemon wheels

1. In a large pitcher filled with ice cubes, combine all the ingredients, and give a good mix before serving.

2. Garnish with lemon wheels and serve in your glassware of choice.

# The Honey Bunny

*Are you ready to party bunny-style? Hop into the world of delightful flavors with this delicious cocktail, featuring a hint of sweetness and garnished with a cute pink marshmallow bunny candy, even the strictest house mother would approve of! So, whether you're hosting a sorority shindig, raising a toast to the sisterhood, or just want to feel as fabulous as Shelley, don your bunny ears and get ready to hop into a night of fun and fabulous drinks!*

**Serves 1**
**Preparation time: 5 minutes**
**Glassware: Rocks glass**

1 ½ ounces (45 milliliters) honey-infused bourbon

½ ounce (30 milliliters) fresh lemon juice

½ ounce (30 milliliters) honey syrup (see page 11)

Ice cubes

*Garnish:* Lemon twist and a pink marshmallow bunny candy

1. Combine all the ingredients in a cocktail shaker along with a handful of ice cubes and shake vigorously until the mixture is cool.

2. Carefully strain the cocktail into a rocks glass filled with ice cubes.

3. Garnish with a lemon twist and a pink marshmallow bunny candy on a cocktail stick.

# Delta Nu Daiquiri

*Embrace the spirit of sisterhood with our Delta Nu Daiquiri, inspired by the iconic sisterhood of Legally Blonde's Delta Nu sorority! This luscious strawberry daiquiri captures the vibrant energy and camaraderie of Elle Woods and her fellow Delta Nu sisters. Pledge allegiance to this delectable cocktail and you won't be disappointed!*

**Serves 2**
**Preparation time: 10 minutes**
**Glassware: Coupes**

2 cups (400 grams) fresh strawberries, hulled and sliced

4 ounces (30 milliliters) light rum

2 ounces (60 milliliters) fresh lime juice

1 ounce (30 milliliters) simple syrup (see page 11)

Ice cubes

*Garnish:* Strawberry halves

1. In a blender combine the fresh strawberries, light rum, fresh lime juice, simple syrup, and two handfuls of ice cubes. Blend until smooth.

2. Carefully pour the cocktail into coupes and garnish each with a strawberry half.

# TEARJERKER TIPPLES

Sometimes there is nothing more cathartic than putting on a sad movie and having a good cry, whether it's Leonardo DiCaprio vanishing into the sea at the end of *Titanic*, Jake Gyllenhaal saying "I wish I knew how to quit you" in *Brokeback Mountain*, or a certain loveable Labrador puppy in *Marley & Me* whose paw prints are etched on all our hearts.

The cocktails featured in this chapter are all based on some of the most tear-inducing chick flicks ever screened. From the heartbreaking romance of *The Notebook* and *The Fault in Your Stars* to the infuriating romance of *10 Things I Hate About You* and the moving ballad of *A Star Is Born*, these movies will get you blubbering every single time. So, get your tissues ready, put on some comfy pjs, pour yourself a tipple or two, and prepare for all the sobbing.

# Love Letter

This cocktail inspired by The Notebook is the perfect accompaniment to shedding a tear as you watch Allie and Noah's enduring romance. Just as their love transcends time, so will your love for this cocktail! A flawless fusion of botanical gin, the subtle elegance of elderflower, and the irresistible sweetness of raspberry syrup.

**Serves 1**
**Preparation: 5 minutes**
**Glassware: Coupe**

1 ½ ounces (45 milliliters) gin

½ ounce (15 milliliters) elderflower liqueur

½ ounce (15 milliliters) fresh lemon juice

½ ounce (15 milliliters) raspberry syrup (see page 13)

Ice cubes

Sparkling wine (to top up)

*Garnish:* Edible rose petals

1. Combine the gin, elderflower liqueur, fresh lemon juice, and raspberry syrup in a cocktail shaker along with a handful of ice cubes and shake vigorously until the mixture is cool.

2. Carefully strain the cocktail into a coupe.

3. Top with sparkling wine and garnish with a scattering of edible rose petals.

# Born Star Martini

*Elevate your senses with this enchanting A Star Is Born–inspired passion fruit martini, a tribute to the fiery passion that ignited between Jackson (Bradley Cooper) and Ally (Lady Gaga). This cocktail is an exotic mix of fruity exuberance with a touch of lime juice, creating a bittersweet symphony of flavors. So, dive into the deep end and unleash your inner pop star with this chart-topping cocktail.*

**Serves 2**
**Preparation time: 5 minutes**
**Glassware: Martini glass**

2 ripe passion fruits

2 ounces (60 milliliters) vanilla vodka

1 ounce (30 milliliters) passion fruit liqueur

½ ounce (15 milliliters) fresh lime juice

½ ounce (15 milliliters) passion fruit syrup (see page 14)

Ice cubes

Prosecco (to top up)

*Garnish:* Halved passion fruit

1. Scoop the seeds from the passion fruits into the can of a cocktail shaker.

2. Next add the vodka, passion fruit liqueur, lime juice, and passion fruit syrup.

3. Combine with a handful of ice cubes and shake vigorously until the mixture is cool.

4. Strain into two martini glasses before topping up with prosecco and garnishing each with a passion fruit half.

# Drink, Pray, Love

While you may not be able to travel to the charming streets of Rome, visit the vivid depths of India, or explore in the tranquil beauty of Bali, this enchanting cocktail is designed to transport you there in spirit. Inspired by Elizabeth Gilbert's transformative journey of self-discovery in Eat, Pray, Love, this indulgent cocktail is perfectly paired with a sweet treat or two. So, sprinkle on some self-love as you sip this cocktail and ponder the true pursuit of happiness, all from the comfort of your own home.

**Serves: 1**
**Preparation time: 5 minutes**
**Glassware: Coupe**

1 tablespoon maple syrup for decorating the glass

3 ounces (90 milliliters) Tequila Rose

1 ounce (30 milliliters) vanilla vodka

Dash rose water

*Garnish:* Pink sprinkles and edible rose petals

1. Rim the coupe (learn how to rim a glass on page 5) with maple syrup and pink sprinkles.

2. Combine the Tequila Rose, vanilla vodka, and dash of rose water in a cocktail shaker along with a handful of ice cubes and shake vigorously until the mixture is cool.

3. Carefully strain the mixture into the coupe and garnish with edible rose petals.

# About Thyme

It's about time you discovered a new favorite cocktail, and this could be it! This botanical blend combines floral elderflower, aromatic thyme, and sweet honey syrup to create a perfectly balanced cocktail. Inspired by the timeless love story between Mary and Tim in the Richard Curtis film About Time, each sip transports you to the heart of the English Cornish countryside, echoing the picturesque backdrop of the film.

**Serves 1**
**Preparation time: 10 minutes**
**Glassware: Coupe**

1 ounce (30 milliliters) gin

½ ounce (15 milliliters) elderflower liqueur

½ ounce (15 milliliters) fresh lemon juice

¼ ounce (7.5 milliliters) thyme syrup (see page 13)

2 ounces (60 milliliters) pink grapefruit juice

2–3 Fresh thyme sprigs

Ice cubes

*Garnish:* lemon twist and thyme sprig

1. Combine the gin, elderflower liqueur, fresh lemon juice, thyme syrup, and pink grapefruit juice in a shaker along with a handful of ice cubes and shake vigorously until the mixture is cool.

2. Strain the cocktail into a coupe and garnish the cocktail with a lemon twist and a fresh thyme sprig.

# Star-Crossed Sippers

The Star-Crossed Sipper is a tribute to the poignant romance of The Fault in Our Stars. With a rim of salt to echo the saltiness of tears shed in this tragic love story, this libation begins as a serene blue, courtesy of butterfly pea flower extract. As you sip, recalling the tender moments of Gus and Hazel's journey, add a shot of lemon juice and watch as the drink transforms into a vibrant purple. Like the star-crossed lovers, recline with this cocktail in hand, gaze upon the night sky, and cherish the fleeting beauty of life and love under the stars.

**Serves 1**
**Preparation time: 5 minutes**
**Glassware: Coupe and shot glass**

Salt, to rim glass

1¾ ounces (50 milliliters) tequila

⅞ ounce (25 milliliters) triple sec

2–3 tablespoons (10–15 drops) butterfly pea flower extract

Pinch edible glitter

Ice cubes

⅞ ounce (25 milliliters) fresh lemon juice

1. Rim a coupe with salt (learn how to rim a glass on page 5).

2. In a cocktail shaker, combine the tequila, triple sec, butterfly pea flower extract, and a pinch of edible glitter along with a handful of ice cubes.

3. Shake until cool, then strain into the rimmed coupe.

4. Next, squeeze the fresh lemon juice into a shot glass. When you want to show off the cocktail's color-changing properties, pour it in. (The butterfly pea flower extract works as a natural pH indicator and will react to the increase in acidity from the lemon juice by changing the color of the drink!)

# Dark 'n' Stormy Romance

*This cocktail is a tantalizing tribute to the classic chick flick 10 Things I Hate About You. Just like the thin line between love and hate explored in the movie, this cocktail balances the intensity of dark rum with the fiery kick of ginger beer, creating a stormy yet irresistibly alluring blend. Despite the stormy exterior, this cocktail guarantees a love affair with every sip, promising to captivate your heart and leave you craving more.*

**Serves 1**
**Preparation time: 5 minutes**
**Glassware: Collins glass**

Ice cubes

1¾ ounces (50 milliliters) dark rum

½ ounce (15 milliliters) fresh lime juice

¼ ounce (7.5 milliliters) simple syrup (see page 11)

Chilled ginger beer (to top up)

*Garnish:* Lime wedge

1. Fill a collins glass with a handful of ice and combine the rum, lime juice, and simple syrup.

2. Top up with ginger beer and stir gently. Garnish with a wedge of lime.

# SIPPING THROUGH THE SILVER SCREEN

Indulge in the charm and nostalgia of classic chick flicks with this dedicated chapter, curated for those timeless films you just can't resist watching again and again. Whether you're in the mood for a sip of romance or a gulp of nostalgia, rest assured, there's a cocktail here to cater to every palate.

Each concoction has been meticulously crafted to capture the essence of these cinematic gems, seamlessly blending classic flavors with a contemporary twist, mirroring the everlasting allure of these beloved movies.

From the sophisticated allure of *Breakfast at Tiffany's* to the rebellious energy of *The Breakfast Club* and the sultry dance floors of *Dirty Dancing*, each cocktail beckons you to relive those unforgettable scenes and films you have been meaning to rewatch. Sit back, unwind, and allow these expertly crafted cocktails to whisk you away on a journey through the magic of cinema.

# Rodeo Drive Dream

To miss out on this cocktail would be a "Big Mistake. Huge!" as Vivian would say. This *Pretty Woman*–inspired concoction is a luxurious and effervescent blend of citrus notes and sweetness, reminiscent of the bubbly Beverly Hills lifestyle and the high-end shopping experiences from the classic film. Imagine sipping this elegant cocktail in a very posh Beverly Hills changing room—after putting the snobby sales assistant in their place, of course! Top off this cocktail with champagne for an extra touch of elegance.

**Serves 1**
**Preparation: 5 minutes**
**Glassware: Champagne flute**

½ ounce (15 milliliters) lemon vodka

2 ounces (60 milliliters) pink lemonade

Pink champagne (to top up)

*Garnish:* Fresh raspberries, lemon wheel, and a dusting of edible gold leaf

1. In a chilled champagne flute, combine the lemon vodka and the pink champagne. Top up with chilled pink champagne.

2. Garnish with fresh raspberries, a lemon wheel, and a dusting of edible gold leaf for that extra-elegant Beverly Hills touch.

# Breakfast at Tiffany's Mimosa

*Transport yourself to the glamor and sophistication of Holly Golightly's world with the Breakfast at Tiffany's Mimosa. Inspired by the iconic film Breakfast at Tiffany's, this cocktail is a true embodiment of style, grace, and timeless beauty. With a beautiful blue hue, reminiscent of Tiffany's signature color, it's a light and refreshing drink with a hint of citrus that you can enjoy while watching Breakfast at Tiffany's or at any stylish gathering.*

**Serves 1**
**Preparation: 5 minutes**
**Glassware: Champagne flute**

½ ounce (15 milliliters) elderflower liqueur

½ ounce (15 milliliters) blue curaçao

Splash orange juice

Champagne or sparkling wine (to top up)

*Garnish:* Orange twist and a Tiffany's cream ribbon

1. Combine the elderflower liqueur, blue curaçao, and a splash of orange juice in a cocktail shaker along with a handful of ice cubes and shake vigorously until the mixture is cool.

2. Strain the cocktail into a chilled champagne flute and top up with champagne/sparkling wine.

3. Garnish with an orange twist and a cream-colored ribbon as the base of the champagne flute to resemble the iconic Tiffany's ribbon.

# Baby's Watermelon Daiquiri

*Sip on this delicious concoction and let it transport you back to the sun-drenched days at Kellerman's Resort, where Baby learned to embrace her passions and follow her heart. Whether you're lounging by the pool or kicking up your heels on the dance floor, this cocktail is sure to keep you refreshed and energized all summer long!*

**Serves 2**
**Preparation time: 10 minutes**
**Glassware: Coupes**

2 cups (400 grams) fresh watermelon, cubed

4 ounces (30 milliliters) light rum

2 ounces (60 milliliters) fresh lime juice

1 ounce (30 milliliters) simple syrup (see page 11)

Ice cubes

*Garnish:* Watermelon wedges and mint sprigs

1. In a blender combine the fresh watermelon, light rum, fresh lime juice, simple syrup, and two handfuls of ice cubes. Blend until smooth.

2. Carefully pour the cocktail into coupes and garnish each with watermelon wedges and mint sprigs.

# Dirty Dance Martini

*No one puts Baby in a corner, and especially not if she's sipping on the Dirty Dance Martini. This cocktail captures the passion and energy of the film's iconic dance moves. So, get ready to have the time of your life with this timeless tipple.*

**Serves 1**
**Preparation time: 5 minutes**
**Glassware: Martini glass**

2 ounces (60 milliliters) vodka

½ ounce (15 milliliters) dry vermouth

½ ounce (15 milliliters) olive brine

Ice cubes

*Garnish:* Cocktail stick and olive

1. In a cocktail shaker, combine the vodka, dry vermouth, and olive brine with a handful of ice and shake vigorously until the mixture is cool.

2. Carefully strain the cocktail into a martini glass and garnish with olive on a cocktail stick.

# Breakfast Clover Club Cocktail

The Breakfast Clover Club Cocktail is specially crafted for all those who are rebellious teenagers at heart and may have earned the occasional detention back in the day! This cocktail is a blend of sweet pink raspberry syrup reminiscent of princess Claire, the bold spirit of gin reflecting rebel John, and the zesty lemon juice representing outcast Allison. When mixed together, it's a winning combination. Served up with a soundtrack showcasing the very best of the eighties, this cocktail will have you raising your fist to the sky in triumph for crafting such a delicious drink!

**Serves 1**
**Preparation time: 10 minutes**
**Glassware: Coupe**

¾ ounce (25 milliliters) raspberry syrup (see page 13)

1¾ ounces (50 milliliters) gin

¾ ounce (25 milliliters) fresh lemon juice

½ ounce (15 milliliters) egg white

Ice cubes

*Garnish:* Three fresh raspberries on cocktail stick

1. Combine the raspberry syrup, gin, lemon juice, and egg white in a cocktail shaker along with a handful of ice cubes. Shake until cold and the egg white is frothy.

2. Carefully strain the mixture into a coupe. Garnish with fresh raspberries on a cocktail stick.

# Fizzy Miss Lizzy

*Inspired by the spirited Elizabeth Bennet from the classic Pride and Prejudice, this lavender-infused concoction is a delightful ode to her charm and elegance. Perfect for refreshing yourself on a hot summer's day or when the thought of Mr. Darcy emerging from the lake gets you feeling a bit flustered. Prepare to be whisked away on a Regency fantasy with this scandalously delicious cocktail.*

**Serves 1**
**Preparation time: 15 minutes**
**Glassware: Coupe**

2 ounce (60 milliliters) lavender-infused gin

½ ounce (15 milliliters) triple sec

½ ounce (15 milliliters) fresh lemon juice

1 ounce (30 milliliters) lavender syrup (see page 12)

Sparkling wine/prosecco (to top up)

Ice cubes

*Garnish:* Lavender sprig

1. Prepare the lavender syrup.

2. Combine the lavender gin, triple sec, fresh lemon juice, and lavender syrup in a cocktail shaker along with a handful of ice cubes and shake vigorously until the mixture is cool.

3. Carefully strain the cocktail into a coupe and top off with sparkling wine/prosecco.

4. Garnish with a lavender sprig.

# Pretty in Drink

*Get ready to add a dash of eighties charm and elegance to your evening with the Pretty in Drink cocktail. Inspired by the iconic film* Pretty in Pink, *this cocktail is a vibrant and visually stunning concoction that captures the essence of youthful romance and timeless style. This delightful fusion of fruity and citrusy notes offers a refreshing and sweet taste that'll make your taste buds dance just like the film's memorable soundtrack.*

**Serves 1**
**Preparation time: 5 minutes**
**Glassware: Coupe**

2 ounces (60 milliliters) raspberry vodka

1 ounce (30 milliliters) peach schnapps

1 ounce (30 milliliters) cranberry juice

½ ounce (15 milliliters) fresh lemon juice

½ ounce (15 milliliters) grenadine

Ice cubes

*Garnish:* Raspberry and lemon twist

1. Combine the raspberry vodka, peach schnapps, juices, and grenadine in a cocktail shaker along with a handful of ice cubes. Shake vigorously until the mixture is cool.

2. Carefully strain the mixture into a coupe. Garnish with a fresh raspberry and a lemon twist on a cocktail stick.

# Moonstruck Moonshine

*This delightful concoction is inspired by the romantic charm of the film Moonstruck starring the truly fabulous diva extraordinaire Cher! The cocktail combines the powerful blend of moonshine with the sweet allure of fresh strawberries, creating a symphony of flavors that will transport you to the moonlit streets of Brooklyn. Just like the characters in the film, who find themselves swept up in the magic of the moonlight, this cocktail is sure to inspire moments of whimsy and wonder. So, whether you're sharing a drink with a loved one or embarking on your own moonstruck adventure, let this cocktail be your guide to a night filled with passion, laughter, and a touch of lunacy.*

**Serves 1**
**Preparation time: 5 minutes**
**Glassware: Collins glass**

2 ounces (60 milliliters) moonshine

1 ounce (40 grams) strawberry jam

½ ounce (15 milliliters) fresh lemon juice

Ice cubes

Club soda (to top up)

*Garnish:* Strawberry half

1. Combine the moonshine, strawberry jam, and lemon juice in a cocktail shaker along with a handful of ice cubes and shake vigorously until the mixture is cool.

2. Fill a collins glass with ice cubes and pour in the cocktail mixture. Top the glass up with club soda and give the cocktail a good stir with a bar spoon.

3. Garnish with a strawberry half.

# Splash Mermaid Cocktail

*Dive into the depths of flavor with the enchanting Splash Mermaid Cocktail, a libation inspired by the beloved eighties film Splash. Concocted with premium coconut rum, smooth vodka, and tangy blue curaçao, this mesmerizing concoction evokes the allure of a tropical blue lagoon. Served in a chilled glass adorned with shimmering blue sugar crystals and a delicate mermaid tail stirrer, each sip transports you to Madison's underwater world. Whether you're hosting a beach party, lounging poolside, or simply daydreaming of adventure, this cocktail is guaranteed to make a splash!*

**Serves 1**
**Preparation time: 5 minutes**
**Glassware: Hurricane glass**

1 ½ ounces (45 milliliters) coconut rum

1 ounce (30 milliliters) vodka

1 ounce (30 milliliters) blue curaçao

2 ounces (60 milliliters) pineapple juice

Lime soda (to top up)

Ice cubes

*Garnish:* Sugar and a mermaid stirrer

1. Fill a hurricane glass with crushed ice.

2. Rim the glass with water and sugar (learn how to rim a glass on page 5).

3. In a cocktail shaker combine the rum, vodka, blue curaçao, and pineapple juice along with a handful of ice cubes and shake vigorously until the mixture is cool.

4. Carefully strain the mixture into the prepared rimmed glass, before topping up with lime soda.

5. Garnish with a mermaid cocktail stirrer.

# LEADING LADIES LIBATIONS

This next chapter is dedicated to the unforgettable women of cinema who inspire us to embrace our own wild adventures. From the high-powered world of fashion in *The Devil Wears Prada* to the fierce spirit in *Miss Congeniality* and the crazy escapades of *Girls Trip*, this chapter celebrates the diverse and dynamic leading ladies, blending their spirit with actual spirits to serve up some Oscar-worthy cocktails!

The cocktails in this chapter are perfectly crafted to accompany you on your own journey, wherever it may lead, whether you're gearing up for a night of dancing on bar tops like the fearless women of *Coyote Ugly* or seeking an indulgent cocktail to enhance a girly shopping trip channeling the spirit of Rebecca Bloomwood from *Confessions of a Shopaholic*. Here's to celebrating the wild, wonderful world of chick flicks and the incredible women who steal the spotlight.

# Miss CongenialiTEA

Step into the world of espionage and glamor with this dazzling makeover of the classic Long Island iced tea. While it may appear tall, sleek, and unsuspicious, don't be fooled—the Miss CongenialiTEA is fully loaded and ready for action. With a blend of vodka, rum, gin, tequila, and triple sec, it's armed to the teeth with spirits! So, gather up your gal pals, don your tiaras, and prepare for an action-packed night as you sip on this potent elixir. Just one glass of The Miss CongenialiTEA and you'll be ready to take on the world—or at least the dance floor.

**Serves 1**
**Preparation time: 5 minutes**
**Glassware: Hurricane glass**

½ ounce (15 milliliters) light rum

½ ounce (15 milliliters) gin

½ ounce (15 milliliters) vodka

½ ounce (15 milliliters) silver tequila

½ ounce (15 milliliters) triple sec

½ ounce (15 milliliters) simple syrup (see page 11)

½ ounce (15 milliliters) fresh lemon juice

½ ounce (15 milliliters) fresh lime juice

Carbonated cola (to top up)

Ice cubes

*Garnish:* Mint sprig and lemon wheel

1. Combine the alcohols, simple syrup, and juices in a cocktail shaker. Shake until cool, then strain into a collins glass and top with cola.

2. Garnish with a mint sprig and a lemon wheel.

# Confessions of a Chocoholic

*After a day of retail therapy, this chocolaty concoction serves as the perfect pick-me-up, offering a luxurious escape from the hustle and bustle of the shopping scene. This decadent libation is more than just a cocktail—it's a dessert in a glass, with velvety chocolate ganache and a hint of vanilla for added depth. Garnished with a dusting of grated chocolate, this cocktail is not just in fashion—it's a style statement. After all, indulgence is always in vogue.*

**Serves 2**
**Preparation time: 45 minutes**
**Glassware: Martini glass**

**For the chocolate ganache:**

8 ounces (230 milliliters) heavy cream

5 ounces (140 grams) semisweet chocolate, chopped

**For the cocktail:**

4 tablespoons grated chocolate, to rim and garnish

10 ounces (300 milliliters) chocolate ganache

2 ounces (60 milliliters) vanilla vodka

2 ounces (60 milliliters) Irish cream

Ice cubes

*Garnish:* Chocolate syrup and grated chocolate

1. Place the martini glasses in a freezer to chill.

2. Drizzle chocolate syrup along the inside of each chilled martini glass, swirling to create a decorative pattern. Return the glasses to the freezer to set.

3. To make the ganache, heat the heavy cream in a saucepan over a medium heat until it starts to simmer. Then, pour the heavy cream over the chopped chocolate in a medium-sized bowl and stir until the chocolate melts. Allow to fully cool before adding to the cocktail to avoid the mixture splitting.

4. Next, combine the chocolate ganache, vodka, and Irish cream in a cocktail shaker along with a handful of ice cubes and shake vigorously until the mixture is cool.

5. Carefully strain the cocktails in the prepared chilled martini glasses. Garnish each with a dusting of grated chocolate.

# Haute Couture Cocktail

*Inspired by the classic Paradise cocktail, this designer libation is the ultimate accessory that would even earn Miranda Priestly's approval in The Devil Wears Prada. Whether you're sipping it at a chic soirée or indulging after a day in the fast-paced fashion world, the Haute Couture Cocktail is your ticket to a luxurious, high-end escape.*

**Serves 1**
**Preparation time: 5 minutes**
**Glassware: Martini glass**

1 ⅓ ounces (40 milliliters) gin

½ ounce (15 milliliters) orange juice

⅔ ounce (20 milliliter) apricot brandy

Ice cubes

*Garnish:* Dried apricot on a cocktail stick

1. Combine all the ingredients in a cocktail shaker along with a handful of ice cubes and shake vigorously until the mixture is cool.

2. Carefully strain the cocktail into a martini glass and garnish with a lemon wedge.

# Coyote Ugly Fireball

*Inspired by the electrifying energy of the Coyote Ugly bar, this drink is sure to fire up your night with its blend of spicy and citrusy flavors with a hint of tequila's boldness. Igniting the overproof rum will let loose the fiery spirit of this iconic bar and create a flaming drink everyone will be staring at!*

**Serves 1**
**Preparation: 10 minutes**
**Glassware: Goblet**

1 ½ ounce (45 millimeters) cinnamon whiskey (such as Fireball)

½ ounce (15 millimeters) tequila

½ ounce (15 millimeters) triple sec

1 ounce (30 millimeters) fresh lime juice

½ ounce (15 millimeters) simple syrup

Dash Tabasco sauce (for that extra kick)

⅕ ounce (6 millimeters) overproof rum

Crushed ice

*Garnish:* Lime wedge and cinnamon stick

1. Combine the cinnamon whiskey, tequila, triple sec, fresh lime juice, simple syrup, and a dash of tabasco sauce in a cocktail shaker along with a handful of ice cubes and shake vigorously until the mixture is cool.

2. Strain the cocktail into a goblet containing crushed ice. Garnish with a lime wedge and cinnamon stick.

3. Carefully add the overproof rum to the surface of the cocktail and ignite.* (See instructions on how to ignite a cocktail safely on page 6.) Remember, do not consume the cocktail until the flame is out.

# Big Easy Elixir

In honor of Regina Hall, Queen Latifah, Tiffany Haddish, and Jada Pinkett Smith—the OG "Flossy Posse" themselves, who embarked on a wild girly getaway to New Orleans in *Girls Trip*—there's no cocktail more fitting to capture the essence of their wild adventure than the iconic Sazerac cocktail. This legendary libation embodies a complex and aromatic symphony of flavors that transports you to the vibrant streets of the French Quarter. Grab some beads and let the good times roll with this powerful little cocktail!

**Serves 1**
**Preparation time: 5 minutes**
**Glassware: Rocks glass**

⅓ ounce (10 milliliters) absinthe

1 sugar cube

2⅓ ounces (70 milliliters) chilled water

3 dashes Peychaud's Bitters

1 dash Angostura bitters

⅔ ounce (20 milliliters) cognac

⅔ ounce (20 milliliters) rye whiskey

Ice cubes

*Garnish:* Lemon twists

1. Rinse a chilled rocks glass with absinthe, discarding any excess, and set aside.

2. In a mixing glass, muddle the sugar cube, water, and the Peychaud's and Angostura bitters.

3. Add the rye and cognac, fill the mixing glass with ice, and stir until well-chilled. Strain into the prepared glass.

4. Twist the lemon peel over the drink's surface to extract the peel's oils, and then garnish with the peel.

# The Mother of All Hangovers

*Inspired by the film Bad Moms, this potent little cocktail will transport you to the world of liberated motherhood! It's time to call up your mom friends, slip into your "sexy bra," and get ready for a wild night where everyone stays up past bedtime! Whether channeling Amy, Carla, or Kiki for a break from parenting chaos, let this pink twist on a Negroni fuel an epic night out. But be warned: its irresistible flavor might lead you to consume one too many, but the dreaded mom hangover is worth the risk for this divine little cocktail.*

**Serves 1**
**Preparation time: 10 minutes**
**Glassware: Rocks glass**

1 ½ ounces (45 milliliters) pink gin

⅔ ounce (20 milliliters) bitter bianco

⅔ ounce (20 milliliters) rosé vermouth

Ice cubes

*Garnish:* Wedge of pink grapefruit

1. Combine the pink gin, bitter, and rosé vermouth in a rocks glass with a small handful of ice. Stir until the outside of the glass feels cold.

2. Garnish with a wedge of pink grapefruit.

# BRIDAL BLENDS

Here, amid the clamor of wedding bells and the promise of eternal love, we invite you to raise a glass and toast to some of the most iconic and heartwarming cinematic moments centered around weddings.

From the bridesmaid adventures of Jane Nichols in *27 Dresses* to the vibrant celebrations of cultural love in *My Big Fat Greek Wedding*, and the uproarious antics of the best friends in *Bridesmaids*, this chapter pays homage to the joy, laughter, and occasional chaos that accompany the journey to the altar.

Featuring classic cocktails with a modern twist to innovative creations inspired by the rich tapestry of wedding traditions around the world, each drink in this chapter is crafted to evoke the romance and nostalgia of your favorite wedding-themed chick flick. So, whether you're dreaming of your own walk down the aisle or simply reveling in the joy of cinematic love stories, let these "Bridal Blends" whisk you away to a cocktail-filled happy-ever-after.

# Marry Me Martini

The Marry Me Martini is inspired by the romantic escapades of Mary Fiore in the beloved rom-com The Wedding Planner. Just as Mary unexpectedly finds herself falling for the groom whose wedding she's orchestrating, you too will be irresistibly drawn to the allure of this enchanting cocktail. Pour yourself a glass and surrender to the romance of this unforgettable cocktail. After all, just like Mary Fiore, you never know where love may lead you.

**Serves 1**
**Preparation time: 5 minutes**
**Glassware: Martini glass**

1 tablespoon maple syrup for decorating the glass

1 ½ ounces (45 milliliters) vanilla vodka

1 ½ ounces (45 milliliters) coconut rum

2 ounces (60 milliliters) coconut cream

½ ounce (15 milliliters) pineapple juice

Ice cubes

*Garnish:* Dried coconut for rimming the glass and white marshmallows

1. Rim the glass with maple syrup and dried coconut (learn how to rim a glass on page 5).

2. In a cocktail shaker, combine the vodka, rum, coconut cream, and pineapple juice with a handful of ice and shake vigorously until the mixture is cool.

3. Carefully strain the cocktail into the prepared martini glass and garnish with white marshmallow.

# Tall, Dark, and Handsome

*Swoon over this irresistible creation, the Tall, Dark and Handsome cocktail, inspired by the romantic comedy charm of The Proposal. Just like Margaret in the movie, this charming, handsome cocktail is all part of the master plan. A blend of butterscotch schnapps, dark crème de cacao, velvety vanilla liqueur, and smooth vodka create a decadent base that sets hearts aflutter.*

**Serves 1**
**Preparation time: 5 minutes**
**Glassware: Collins glass**

Ice cubes

½ ounce (15 milliliters) butterscotch schnapps

½ ounce (15 milliliters) dark crème de cacao

½ ounce (15 milliliters) vanilla liqueur

½ ounce (15 milliliters) vodka

Carbonated cola (to top up)

*Garnish:* Chocolate syrup

1. Fill a collins glass with ice cubes and pour in the alcohol. Top the glass up with cola and give the cocktail a good stir with a bar spoon.

2. Garnish with a drizzle of chocolate syrup.

# Blushing Bridesmaids

This *Bridesmaids*-inspired cocktail is a must for any bachelorette bash, especially one destined for unforgettable, cringeworthy moments! Crafted with smooth vodka and pomegranate liqueur, its rosy hue reflects the blushing bride herself. So, pop open a bottle and celebrate in style! Just take a lesson from Annie's mishaps and steer clear of any dubious meat kebabs.

**Serves 1**
**Preparation time: 5 minutes**
**Glassware: Champagne glass**

1 ounce (30 milliliters) vodka

½ ounce (15 milliliters) pomegranate liqueur

½ ounce (15 milliliters) simple syrup (see page 11)

Dash rose water

Sparkling rosé (to top up)

Ice cubes

*Garnish:* Pomegranate seeds

1. Combine the vodka, pomegranate liqueur, simple syrup, and a dash of rose water in a cocktail shaker along with a handful of ice cubes. Shake vigorously until the mixture is cool.

2. Carefully strain the cocktail into a champagne glass and top up with sparkling rosé.

3. Garnish with a few pomegranate seeds.

# Crazy Rich Libation

*Step into the world of extravagance and opulence with this sensational creation, the Crazy Rich Libation. Inspired by the lavish lifestyles depicted in the movie Crazy Rich Asians, this cocktail is a decadent delight that transports you to the glittering streets of Singapore. Created with premium ingredients, including top-shelf vodka, exotic lychee liqueur, and lime juice, the Crazy Rich Libation is a symphony of flavors that will leave you feeling like a million bucks. So, whether you're sipping poolside at a lavish mansion or mingling at a soirée, this is the perfect accessory for living your most extravagant life.*

**Serves 1**
**Preparation time: 5 minutes**
**Glassware: Martini glass**

1 ½ ounces (45 milliliters) vodka

1 ounce (30 milliliters) lychee liqueur

½ ounce (15 milliliters) fresh lime juice

½ ounce (15 milliliters) simple syrup (see page 11)

Pinch edible gold glitter

Ice cubes

*Garnish:* Fresh lychee fruit rolled in edible gold glitter on a cocktail stick

1. Combine the vodka, lychee liqueur, lime juice, simple syrup, and a pinch of edible gold glitter in a cocktail shaker along with a handful of ice cubes. Shake vigorously until the mixture is cool.

2. Carefully strain the mixture into a martini glass. Garnish with a peeled lychee fruit rolled in edible gold glitter on a cocktail stick.

# Bollywood Marital Bliss

*Experience the dazzling allure of Bollywood with this sensational cocktail inspired by the vibrant energy of the film Bride and Prejudice. This spiced concoction captures the essence of Bollywood's glitz and glam, transporting you to a world of romance and excitement. The Bollywood Marital Bliss blends spiced rum with a splash of exotic mango juice, infused with a medley of warm aromatic spices like cardamom, cloves, and a hint of ginger. Served in a chilled glass rimmed with gold glitter and garnished with a vibrant edible flower, this cocktail is a visual masterpiece that exudes elegance and sophistication.*

**Serves 1**
**Preparation time: 5 minutes**
**Glassware: Coupe**

1 ½ ounces (45 milliliters) spiced rum

2 ounces (60 milliliters) mango juice

½ ounce (15 milliliters) simple syrup (see page 11)

¼ teaspoon ground cardamom

Pinch ground cloves

Pinch ground ginger

Ice cubes

*Garnish:* Edible gold glitter for rimming the glass and edible flowers

1. Rim the coupe using water and edible gold glitter (learn how to rim a glass on page 5).

2. Combine the spiced rum, mango juice, simple syrup, and spices in a cocktail shaker along with a handful of ice cubes and shake vigorously until the mixture is cool.

3. Carefully strain the mixture into a prepared coupe. Garnish with edible flowers.

# My Big Fat Greek Koktail

*Join in with the Portokalos family festive celebrations with this Mediterranean-inspired cocktail. Embodying the spirit of Greek hospitality and familial celebration, this cocktail blends the bold essence of Greek ouzo with the zesty freshness of lemon juice and sweetness from the honey syrup. Each sip transports you to the vibrant festivities of a Greek wedding, so raise your glasses and toast the happy couple. OPA!*

**Serves 1**
**Preparation time: 10 minutes**
**Glassware: Collins glass**

2½ ounces (75 milliliters) ouzo

½ ounce (15 milliliters) fresh lemon juice

¼ ounce (7.5 milliliters) honey syrup (see page 11)

Ice cubes

*Garnish:* Lemon twist and thyme sprig

1. Combine the ouzo, fresh lemon juice, and honey syrup in a cocktail shaker along with a handful of ice cubes. Shake vigorously until the mixture is cool.

2. Strain the cocktail into a collins glass filled with ice and garnish the cocktail with a lemon twist and a fresh thyme sprig.

# Mint to Be

*Savor the exquisite flavors of the Mint to Be mojito, a tantalizing creation inspired
by the romantic comedy gem, 27 Dresses. Just as Jane discovered her perfect match
amid a whirlwind of weddings, this cocktail promises to be your ideal companion.
With its seamless fusion of succulent strawberries and refreshing mint, each sip is
a union of flavors that's simply divine. Some cocktails, like some love stories, are
undeniably meant to be.*

**Serves 1**
**Preparation time: 5 minutes**
**Glassware: Collins glass**

5–6 fresh strawberries,
  hulled and sliced

6–8 mint leaves

2 ounces (60 milliliters)
  light rum

1 ounce (30 milliliters)
  fresh lime juice

1 ounce (30 milliliters)
  honey syrup (see
  page 11)

Soda water (to top up)

Ice cubes

*Garnish:* Mint sprig,
  strawberries, and
  lime slice

1. In a sturdy glass or cocktail shaker, place
   the strawberries and fresh mint leaves.
   Muddle the ingredients to release their
   flavors.

2. Add the muddled ingredients to the glass
   and fill with ice cubes, almost to the top.

3. Next combine the light rum, lime juice,
   and honey syrup. Using a cocktail
   stirrer or a long spoon, gently mix the
   ingredients together.

4. Top up the glass with soda water before
   garnishing with a sprig of mint, a slice of
   lime, and a whole strawberry or two.

# MUSICAL MIXOLOGY

Welcome to the enchanting world of "Musical Mixology"! This chapter celebrates the magic of song with a collection of cocktails inspired by some of the most iconic musical films of all time. From the sun-drenched shores of Greece in *Mamma Mia* to the glittering streets of Hollywood in *La La Land*, get ready to sip your way through a symphony of flavors and melodies that will transport you to another world.

So, grab your cocktail shaker and your favorite soundtrack. Whether you're belting out show tunes with friends or enjoying a cozy movie night at home, these cocktails are sure to hit all the right notes.

# Voulez-Woo

*Are you ready to embark on a musical journey of taste that'll have you saying, "Gimme, gimme, gimme another sip!"? The zesty Voulez-Woo cocktail is a symphony of flavors that'll make you want to dance on the bar, embracing your inner dancing queen!*

**Serves 1**
**Preparation time: 5 minutes**
**Glassware: Martini glass**

1 ounce (30 milliliters) vodka

1 ounce (30 milliliters) peach schnapps

½ ounce (15 milliliters) fresh lime juice

3 ounces (90 milliliters) cranberry juice

Ice cubes

*Garnish:* Lime wedge

1. Combine the vodka, schnapps, lime, and cranberry juice in a cocktail shaker half-filled with ice cubes. Shake until cool, then strain into a martini glass.

2. Garnish with a lime wedge before serving. Take it now or leave it (aha)!

# Pour Myself a Cocktail of Ambition

*This hardworking "9-to-5" cocktail is a delightful mix of bold flavors and a touch of sophistication, just like the three leading ladies of this hit musical! With Tennessee whiskey as a nod to Dolly Parton's Tennessee roots, and a whole lot of coffee, this cocktail will have you dancing as well as plotting the demise of the patriarchy all at the same time.*

**Serves 1**
**Preparation time: 5 minutes**
**Glassware: Martini glass**

2 ounces (60 milliliters) Tennessee whiskey

1 ounce (30 milliliters) coffee liqueur

1¾ ounce (50 milliliters) freshly brewed espresso, cooled

½ ounce (15 milliliters) simple syrup

Dash Angostura bitters

Ice cubes

*Garnish:* Three coffee beans

1. Combine the whiskey, coffee liqueur, simple syrup, and dash of Angostura bitters in a cocktail shaker along with a handful of ice cubes. Shake until cool.

2. Carefully strain the mixture into a martini glass. Garnish with three coffee beans.

# The Corny Collins Cocktail

*Welcome to the vibrant swinging sixties world of Hairspray and add a touch of retro glam to your evening. Whether you're doing the twist, the mashed potato, or the funky chicken, this cocktail is your ultimate dance partner for a night of fun. Gather your friends, tease up your hair to new heights, and prepare to show off your moves on Baltimore's hottest dance show!*

**Serves 1**
**Preparation time: 5 minutes**
**Glassware: Collins glass**

Pomegranate seeds

Rosemary sprig

2 ounces (60 milliliters) port wine

2 ounces (60 milliliters) pomegranate juice

½ ounce (15 milliliters) Fresh lemon juice

½ ounce (15 milliliters) simple syrup (see page 11)

Ice cubes

*Garnish:* Lemon wedge, pomegranate seed, and rosemary sprig

1. In the can of a cocktail shaker muddle a few pomegranate seed and a sprig of rosemary. Add the port wine, pomegranate juice, and simple syrup into a cocktail shaker.

2. Fill up a collins glass with crushed ice and pour in the cocktail mixture.

3. Garnish with a sprinkle of pomegranate seeds and a rosemary sprig.

# Hopelessly Devoted

*Indulge in the nostalgia of the iconic musical Grease and be hopelessly devoted to this electrifying cocktail. This cocktail is a symphony of fruity rhubarb and refreshing flavors perfect for "oh, those summer nights!" Whether you're belting out "We Go Together" or dancing along to "Greased Lightning," this cocktail is sure to get you moving and grooving like a true Pink Lady or T-Bird!*

**Serves 1**
**Preparation: 5 minutes**
**Glassware: Wineglass**

1½ ounce (45 milliliters) rhubarb liqueur/ rhubarb gin

3–4 fresh raspberries

4 ounces (120 milliliters) soda water

Sparkling rosé (to top up)

*Garnish:* Fresh raspberries and 2–3 mint leaves

1. In the base of the cocktail shaker, muddle the fresh raspberries until they release their juice.

2. Add the rhubarb liqueur into the cocktail shaker along with a handful of ice cubes. Shake vigorously until the mixture is cool.

3. Carefully strain the mixture into a wineglass filled with a few ice cubes. Pour in the soda water and then top up the glass with sparkling rosé.

4. Garnish with fresh raspberries and 2–3 mint leaves.

# Channing TateRUM

*Presenting the Channing TateRUM—a flirtatiously delicious concoction inspired by the tantalizing charm and moves of Magic Mike. This cocktail is a sultry blend of smooth rum and a touch of sweetness that'll make your taste buds dance with delight, just like Channing Tatum's irresistible moves. It's the perfect drink to sip while watching the film with your gal pals, or better yet, while partying and showing off your own sexy moves!*

**Serves 1**
**Preparation time: 5 minutes:**
**Glassware: Martini glass**

2 ounces (60 milliliters) dark rum

1 ounce (30 milliliters) pineapple juice

½ ounce (15 milliliters) fresh lime juice

½ ounce (15 milliliters) grenadine

Pinch edible glitter

Ice cubes

*Garnish:* Pineapple wedge, edible glitter, and a glittery bow tie

1. Rim the glass using water and edible glitter (learn how to rim a glass on page 5).

2. Combine the rum, juices, and grenadine in a cocktail shaker along with a handful of ice cubes. Shake vigorously until the mixture is cool.

3. Carefully strain the mixture into the prepared martini glass and garnish with a pineapple wedge and tie a signature glittery bow tie on the stem of the glass.

# Hollywood Hits

*Step into the spotlight and indulge in the Hollywood Hits cocktail, a tribute to the timeless allure of the film La La Land, in which dreams take center stage and love stories unfold amid the glittering lights of Tinseltown. Garnished with a playful touch of popcorn, this cocktail is the ultimate companion for a movie night with your very own A-listers. With the Hollywood Hits cocktail in hand, every moment becomes a scene worth savoring.*

**Serves 1**
**Preparation: 5 minutes**
**Glassware: Coupe**

1 ½ ounces (45 milliliters) light rum

⅓ ounce (10 milliliters) pink grapefruit juice

⅙ ounce (5 milliliters) grenadine

⅓ ounce (10 milliliters) simple syrup (see page 11)

⅓ ounce (10 milliliters) egg white

Ice cubes

*Garnish:* Popcorn on a cocktail stick

1. Combine the rum, pink grapefruit, grenadine, simple syrup, and egg white in a cocktail shaker along with a handful of ice cubes. Shake until cold and the egg white is frothy.

2. Carefully strain the mixture into a coupe. Garnish with three pieces of popcorn on a cocktail stick.

# Highball Musical

*Introducing the Highball Musical—a high-energy, showstopping cocktail that's a perfect ode to the hit songs and infectious spirit of all those at East High School. Sip on this sparkling concoction while reminiscing about your favorite High School Musical song and how much you wished you had Sharpay's wardrobe! Whether you're "Breaking Free" or ready to "Get'cha Head in the Game," this whiskey-infused cocktail will have you dancing to the nostalgic rhythm of the Wildcats!*

**Serves 1**
**Preparation: 5 minutes**
**Glassware: Collins glass**

2 ounces (60 milliliters) bourbon

½ ounce (15 milliliters) fresh lemon juice

6 ounces (180 milliliters) ginger ale

Ice cubes

*Garnish:* Lemon twist and 2–3 mint leaves

1. Fill a collins glass with a handful of ice. Add the bourbon and lemon juice. Top up with ginger ale and stir gently.

2. Garnish with a lemon twist and 2 to 3 mint leaves in the glass.

# Rom-Com ✳ ✳
✳ on the Rocks ✳

In this chapter, all the cocktails featured are inspired by the heartwarming, hilarious, and often unpredictable world of romantic comedies. From the golden era for rom-com with films like *When Harry Met Sally* and *There's Something About Mary*, this chapter has the perfect pairing of quirky meet-cute with the perfect cocktail.

Rom-coms nowadays come in all genres to suit all tastes, just like cocktails! So, shake things up with cocktails inspired by the suave charm of *Hitch*, the laid-back country charm of *Sweet Home Alabama*, and the wild antics of the ladies of *Sex in The City*. Whether you're swooning over a handsome stranger, laughing with your best friends, or letting loose on the dance floor, there's a cocktail in this chapter to suit every mood and occasion.

# Alabama Slammer

*Step into the charming world of the deep south with the Alabama Slammer cocktail, inspired by the heartwarming movie Sweet Home Alabama. This cocktail captures the essence of Southern hospitality and the movie's sweet romance, making it the perfect drink for a cozy evening in front of a fire with a good film and good company.*

**Serves 1**
**Preparation time: 5 minutes**
**Glassware: Collins glass**

1 ounce (30 milliliters) Southern Comfort

1 ounce (30 milliliters) almond liqueur

1 ounce (30 milliliters) sloe gin

½ ounce (15 milliliters) orange juice

½ ounce (15 milliliters) fresh lemon juice

Ice cubes

Splash grenadine

*Garnish:* Orange wheel and maraschino cherry

1. Combine the Southern Comfort, almond liqueur, sloe gin, orange juice, and lemon juice in a cocktail shaker along with a handful of ice cubes. Shake vigorously until the mixture is cool.

2. Strain the cocktail into a collins glass and add a splash of grenadine over the back of a spoon, allowing it to settle at the bottom, creating a layered effect.

3. Garnish with an orange wheel and a maraschino cherry.

# There's Something About Bloody Mary

*Crafted with vodka, tangy tomato juice, and a perfectly balanced blend of spices that pack a punch, this cocktail is sure to wake up your taste buds and leave you craving more. Served over ice in a chilled glass, it's as refreshing as it is satisfying—the perfect pick-me-up for the morning after a big party, a brunch date with friends, or a lazy afternoon lounging by the pool. You can rest assured that there will be no hair-raising surprises, only moments to savor and enjoy with this delicious cocktail.*

**Serves 2**
**Preparation: 10 minutes**
**Glassware: Pitcher and mason jars**

3½ ounces (100 milliliters) vodka

17½ ounces (500 milliliters) tomato juice

½ ounce (15 milliliters) fresh lemon juice

Few shakes Worcestershire sauce

Few shakes Tabasco

Pinch celery salt

Pinch black pepper

Crushed ice

*Garnish:* Celery stick and a slice of lemon

1. Place crushed ice in a pitcher and pour the vodka, tomato juice, and lemon juice over the ice.

2. Add the Worcestershire source, Tabasco, celery salt, and pepper. Stir until the outside of the pitcher feels cold.

3. Serve in mason jars and garnish each with a celery stick and a slice of lemon.

# Carrie Me Away

This cocktail is inspired by the adventures of Sex and the City's iconic leading lady, Carrie Bradshaw. Picture yourself sipping on this chic concoction while strolling down Fifth Avenue, channeling Carrie's iconic fashion sense and infectious energy. Mix infused raspberry vodka with cranberry juice, melon liqueur, and fresh lemon juice, just like that, the perfect cocktail that exudes cosmopolitan flair!

**Serves 1**
**Preparation time: 5 minutes**
**Glassware: Coupe**

1 ½ ounces (45 milliliters) raspberry vodka

½ ounce (15 milliliters) melon liqueur

½ ounce (15 milliliters) fresh lemon juice

1 ounce (30 milliliters) cranberry juice

Ice cubes

*Garnish:* Lime wedge

1. Combine the vodka, melon liqueur, and juices in a cocktail shaker along with a handful of ice cubes and shake vigorously until the mixture is cool.

2. Carefully strain the mixture into the coupe and garnish with a lime wedge.

# Made in Manhattan

*The Made in Manhattan is a bourbon twist on the classic cocktail that embodies the resilience and ambition of Marisa Ventura from the heartwarming rom-com Maid in Manhattan. This drink strikes the perfect balance between sweetness and aromatic notes, symbolizing the strength needed to overcome life's struggles and pursue your dreams. As you savor each sip, let it inspire you to carve your own path to success, not letting what other people think hold you back!*

**Serves 1**
**Preparation time: 5 minutes**
**Glassware: Martini glass**

2 ½ ounces (75 milliliters) bourbon

½ ounce (15 milliliters) sweet vermouth

½ ounce (15 milliliters) extra dry vermouth

2 dashes orange bitters

Ice cubes

*Garnish:* Maraschino cherry

1. Combine the bourbon, vermouth, and bitters in a mixing glass with a handful of ice cubes and stir until well chilled.

2. Strain into a martini glass and garnish with a maraschino cherry on a cocktail stick.

# Screaming O

*Inspired by the iconic film* When Harry Met Sally, *indulge in the euphoric combination of rich Irish cream liqueur, velvety coffee liqueur, and smooth vodka, creating a dessert served with a generous mix of innuendo. Just like Sally's unforgettable moment in Katz's Delicatessen, this cocktail will definitely have guests saying, "I'll have what she's having."*

**Serves 1**
**Preparation time: 5 minutes**
**Glassware: Hurricane glass**

1¼ ounces (37.5 milliliters) vodka

1¼ ounces (37.5 milliliters) coffee liqueur

1¼ ounces (37.5 milliliters) amaretto liqueur

1¼ ounces (37.5 milliliters) Irish cream liqueur

1¼ ounces (37.5 milliliters) single cream/half-and-half

1¼ ounces (37.5 milliliters) milk

Ice cubes

Orange juice (to top up)

*Garnish:* Cocoa powder

1. Combine all ingredients in a cocktail shaker along with a handful of ice cubes and shake vigorously until the mixture is cool.

2. Add crushed ice to the hurricane glass and then carefully strain the cocktail into the glass.

3. Garnish with a dusting of cocoa powder.

# Hitch Hooch

This cocktail is as smooth as Mr. Hitch himself, guaranteed to make a lasting impression on everyone who drinks it. So, whether you're out on the town, mingling at a cocktail party, or simply enjoying a quiet evening in, let the Hitch Hooch charm you as you navigate the complexities of modern romance.

**Serves 6**
**Preparation time: 10 minutes**
**Glassware: Large pitcher**

4 ounces (120 milliliters) raspberry vodka

3 ounces (90 milliliters) raspberry sours

1 ounce (30 milliliters) fresh lemon juice

Pink Hooch/pink lemonade (to top up)

Ice cubes

*Garnish:* Lemon wheels, edible bougainvilla petals, and a sprinkling of edible glitter

1. In a larger pitcher filled with ice cubes, combine all the ingredients and mix well before serving.

2. Garnish with lemon wheels, a sprinkling of edible glitter, and serve in your glassware of choice.

# Samantha's Fruity Screwdriver

*Kim Cattrall may not be reprising her role in the reboot (womp, womp), but her epic one-liners will live on forever. "The good ones screw you, the bad ones screw you, and the rest don't know how to screw you," is, perhaps, one of her finest. Therefore, what better way to honor the queen of sassy comebacks than a fruity extra twist on the classic screwdriver cocktail? Depending on how generous your pouring of vodka is, we can guarantee you that this cocktail will absolutely screw you over after a few!*

**Serves 1**
**Preparation time: 5 minutes**
**Glassware: Collins glass**

Ice cubes

2 ounces (60 milliliters)
  vodka

3 dashes orange bitters

2 ounces (60 milliliters)
  orange juice

2 ounces (60 milliliters)
  pineapple juice

*Garnish:* Pineapple leaves

1. Fill a collins glass with ice cubes and pour over the vodka and orange bitters.

2. Top up with the orange and pineapple juice before garnishing with pineapple leaves.

# SEASONAL SIPS

Whether you're snuggled up with your significant other on February 14th, gathering with friends for a bewitching Halloween bash, or decking the halls with boughs of holly, we've got the perfect libations to elevate your festive celebrations.

Just as you have the perfect movie to set the seasonal mood, now you have the perfect cocktail to pair it with! From the swoon-worthy romance of *Valentine's Day* to the spellbinding charm of *Hocus Pocus*, and a Christmas selection box of rom-com classics like *The Holiday* and *Love Actually*, we've carefully curated a selection of drinks guaranteed to get you in the festive spirit.

So put up the decorations, gather your nearest and dearest, and craft some of these cocktails to celebrate. Because after all, what better excuse to have fun and indulge in some delicious drinks than the changing seasons?

# Vodka-Soaked Valentine

*Whether you're celebrating with a special someone or flying solo, indulge in the ultimate treat with this pink variation of the classic mudslide cocktail. Savor the flavor as you lose yourself in the romantic escapades of the star-packed chick flick* Valentine's Day. *And if nothing else, enjoy the iconic Taylor Lautner/Taylor Swift action on-screen—because what could be more of a treat than that?*

**Serves 1**
**Preparation time: 5 minutes**
**Glassware: Martini glass**

5 strawberries, hulled

1 ounce (30 milliliters) coffee liqueur

1 ounce (30 milliliters) vanilla vodka

1 ounce (30 milliliters) Irish cream liqueur

1 scoop vanilla ice cream

Ice cubes

*Garnish:* Whipped cream, sugar hearts, and a fresh raspberry

1. In a blender combine the strawberries, coffee liqueur, vanilla vodka, Irish cream, and ice cream. Blend until smooth.

2. Strain the mixture into a martini glass and garnish with whipped cream, a sprinkling of sugar hearts, and a raspberry on a cocktail stick.

# Hocus Pocus Potion

Step into the mystical world of Sanderson Sisters with this magical Hocus Pocus Potion! Crafted with a dash of enchantment and a sprinkle of nostalgia, this bewitching concoction pays homage to Winifred, Sarah, and Mary, and captures the essence of the beloved movie in every sip. Here's to a night of magic, mischief, and mayhem—just like the best Halloween nights in Salem!

**Serves 4**
**Preparation time: Freeze overnight, 5 minutes**
**Glassware: Cauldron and rocks glasses**

1 (750-milliliter) bottle rosé

2 ounces (60 milliliters) strawberry syrup (see page 12)

2 ounces (60 milliliters) fresh lemon juice

2 ounces (60 milliliters) gin

*Garnish:* Fresh strawberries, halved

1. Pour the rosé into an ice cube tray and freeze overnight.

2. In a blender, combine the rosé ice cubes, strawberry syrup, fresh lemon juice, and gin. Blend for 2 minutes or until smooth.

3. Pour into a cauldron before serving in rocks glasses, each garnished with a halved strawberry.

# The Holiday Snow Globe Spritzer

*This winter wonderland–themed drink pays homage to the heartwarming Christmas movie The Holiday, bringing the spirit of the season to life in a charming snow globe presentation resemblant of the scenes Cameron Diaz in that idyllic snow-dusted English cottage. Allow this cocktail to transport you to a world where holiday miracles are possible, and who knows, this Christmas, Jude Law just might come knocking at your door!*

**Serves 1**
**Preparation time: Freeze overnight, 5 minutes**
**Glassware: Freezer-safe rocks glasses**

## For each snow globe glass:

Small handful of cranberries

1 rosemary sprig, trimmed evenly to resemble a Christmas tree

Tonic water

## For the cocktail:

Tonic water

2 ounces (60 millimeters) gin

½ ounce (15 milliliters) fresh lemon juice

½ ounce (15 milliliters) simple syrup

1. Using freezer-safe rocks glasses, add a small handful of cranberries to each glass.

2. Trim the bottom of a rosemary sprig evenly to resemble a Christmas tree shape. Place it in the middle of the glass upside down, gently pushing it into the cranberries.

3. Fill the glass with roughly 1 inch (2.5 cm) of tonic water, ensuring that the rosemary sprig remains upright. Tie the rosemary sprig with string around the stem and use tape to secure the string to the sides of the glass so the sprig stays upright.

4. Carefully place the glasses in the freezer for at least 45 minutes, or until the water is frozen. This will create the "snow globe" effect.

Ice cubes

Sparkling wine (to top up)

*Garnish:* Rim with
granulated sugar
(optional, for a
snowy effect)

5. If desired, rim (see page 5) the glass using
water and granulated sugar for an extra
snowy effect.

6. Once frozen combine the gin, fresh lemon
juice, and simple syrup in a cocktail
shaker with a handful of ice cubes. Shake
until cool and strain into the prepared
snow globe glasses.

7. Top up each glass with sparkling wine and
serve to guests.

# Bridget's Chocolate Delight

*Bridget Jones once famously said, "Chocolate has the power to fix almost everything. Fact." And that's undeniably true with this indulgent cocoa cocktail! Whether you're struggling to be taken seriously at work or torn between your very own Mark Darcy and Daniel Cleaver, with this chocolate martini in hand, life's problems become just that little bit sweeter! Cozy up in your favorite Christmas sweater, cue up the movie, and indulge in all things Bridget Jones.*

**Serves 1**
**Preparation time: 5 minutes**
**Glassware: Martini glass**

2 ounces (60 milliliters) chocolate liqueur

1 ounce (30 milliliters) vodka

1 ounce (30 milliliters) cream

½ ounce (15 milliliters) vanilla syrup (see page 14)

Ice cubes

*Garnish:* Chocolate syrup and dusting of cocoa powder

1. Combine the chocolate liqueur, vodka, cream, and vanilla syrup in a cocktail shaker along with a handful of ice cubes. Shake vigorously until the mixture is cool.

2. Drizzle some chocolate syrup around the inside of a martini glass, creating a decorative swirl.

3. Carefully strain the mixture into the prepared martini glass. Dust the top of the cocktail with a sprinkle of cocoa powder.

# Naughty and Spice

*It's time to celebrate the ultimate Christmas chick flick in style! In homage to the iconic characters of Love Actually, let's celebrate with not one, but two Christmassy themed cocktails layered in one glass! Whether you find yourself on the Naughty side, akin to Alan Rickman's character Harry, or you're nice with a dash of spice, much like Hugh Grant's prime minister, there's a cocktail crafted just for you. So, whether you're stirring up trouble or spreading cheer, these cocktails are sure to delight all who drink them.*

**Serves 1**
**Preparation time: 5 minutes**
**Glassware: Martini glass**

### For the naughty side:

1 ounce (30 milliliters) spiced rum

½ ounce (15 milliliters) cinnamon schnapps

½ ounce (15 milliliters) ginger liqueur

½ ounce (15 milliliters) honey syrup (see page 11)

Ice cubes

*Garnish:* A pinch of ground cinnamon

1. In a cocktail shaker filled with a handful of ice, combine spiced rum, cinnamon schnapps, ginger liqueur, and honey syrup. Shake vigorously until cool.

2. Strain the mixture into a chilled martini glass.

3. Sprinkle a pinch of ground cinnamon on the surface.

### For the nice side:

1 ounce (30 milliliters) vanilla vodka

½ ounce (15 milliliters) Irish cream liqueur

½ ounce (15 milliliters) white chocolate liqueur

Ice cubes

*Garnish:* Whipped cream and grated white chocolate

1. First, make the Naughty layer (instructions above).

2. In a cocktail shaker filled with a handful of ice, combine vanilla vodka, Irish cream liqueur, and white chocolate liqueur. Shake vigorously until cool.

3. Gently layer (learn how to layer on page 5) the Nice mixture on top of the Naughty layer by pouring it over the back of a spoon.

4. Top off the Nice layer with a dollop of whipped cream and grated white chocolate.

# Blizzard Bliss

The Blizzard Bliss perfectly captures the spirit of exhilaration and relaxation following an adrenaline-pumping day on the slopes. This après-ski delight is a cinematic match made in snowy heaven and pays homage to the charming snow-mantic comedy, Falling for Christmas, starring Lindsay Lohan. Just like the fabulous heiress herself, you might find yourself with a touch of amnesia the morning after indulging in a few of these boozy treats!

**Serves 1**
**Preparation time: 5 minutes**
**Glassware: Goblet**

1 tablespoon maple syrup for decorating the glass

Crushed ice

2 ounces (60 milliliters) pineapple juice

1 ounce (30 milliliters) blue curaçao

1 ounce (30 milliliters) vodka

1 ounce (30 milliliters) cream of coconut

*Garnish:* dried coconut for rimming the glass

1. Rim the glass with maple syrup and dried coconut (learn how to rim a glass on page 5).

2. Next, in a blender, combine two handfuls of crushed ice with the pineapple juice, blue curaçao, vodka, and cream of coconut. Blend the mixture until smooth before serving in the prepared rimmed glass.

# Tipsy All the Way

*Inspired by the heartwarming romantic LGBTQ+ Christmas comedy Single All the Way this festive cocktail is the ideal holiday drink to enjoy while navigating those sometimes-judgmental family gatherings. Whether you're introducing someone special to your family for the first time or simply looking to take the edge off during a bustling family reunion, this cocktail is your perfect companion! Garnished with sugar-frosted cranberries and a fragrant rosemary sprig, this drink looks stunning and is bursting with Christmas cheer.*

**Serves 1**
**Preparation time: 5 minutes**
**Glassware: Coupe**

Handful fresh cranberries

1 ounce (30 milliliters) fresh lime juice

1 ounce (30 milliliters) honey syrup (see page 11)

2 ounce (60 milliliters) silver tequila

Ice cubes

*Garnish*: Granulated sugar, cranberries, and a rosemary sprig

1. Start by preparing the honey syrup.

2. In the can of the cocktail shaker, muddle the cranberries and the honey syrup together.

3. Combine the silver tequila and fresh lime juice in a cocktail shaker with a handful of ice cubes. Shake until the mixture is cool.

4. Strain the cocktail into a coupe.

5. To garnish, dip the cranberries and rosemary sprig into some honey syrup. Place some granulated sugar into a small bowl and dip in the wet cranberries and rosemary sprig and set them aside to dry before decorating the cocktail.

# ACKNOWLEDGMENTS

A special thank-you to Grace Hatley for her incredible artistic flair in cocktail styling throughout this book.

We also want to express our gratitude to our wonderful friends at Balance, especially Chloé, Katie, and Rachael, for their invaluable assistance in creating some of the props and stylings.

# CONVERSION CHART

| Term | Measurement (Imperial) | Measurement (Metric) |
|------|------------------------|----------------------|
| 1 part | Any equal part | Any equal part |
| 1 dash | $\frac{1}{32}$ ounce | 1 milliliter |
| 1 teaspoon | $\frac{1}{5}$ ounce | 6 milliliters |
| 1 tablespoon | $\frac{1}{6}$ ounce | 5 milliliters |
| 1 pony | $\frac{1}{2}$ ounce | 15 milliliters |
| 1 jigger/shot | 1 ounce | 30 milliliters |
| 1 snit | 3 ounces | 90 milliliters |
| 1 wineglass | 4 ounces | 120 milliliters |
| 1 split | 6 ounces | 180 milliliters |
| 1 cup | 8 ounces | 240 milliliters |
| 1 pint | 16 ounces | 475 milliliters |

# ✦ INDEX ✦